*To Rosie - for sharing the j*

CW00417615

Table of contents

Contents

Italy: the rough with the smooth

By David Eidlestein

We witness Carlo's finest hour
Digestivo

Late in 2001 David and Rosie Eidlestein bought a small, derelict farmhouse in the central Italian region of Le Marche. It was intended to be a holiday home where they could escape for occasional breaks from their busy jobs as newspaper editors. In 2002 they decided instead to sell up in England, quit their jobs and move to Italy. It didn't happen quite like that – but they did embark on a 12-year adventure as they divided their lives between the south-west of England and the medieval Italian village of Montottone. This is their story. (Some names have been changed in the interests of preserving friendships).

Marche

Antipasto

Scenario one: It had been a solemn promise. The mayor had looked me straight in the face and given me his word of honour that our battered little road would be resurfaced long before our next visit in a month's time. He would take personal responsibility. We could be absolutely certain that, in a few short weeks, the steep, potholed, rutted, collapsing track which led, eventually, to our property would be fully and beautifully repaired. The *comune* would swing swiftly into action; Giuseppe, the *comune*'s sole employee, would be sent in as soon as he had finished his work driving the school bus. Probably tomorrow.

For a moment, we believed him. *Signor Sindaco* was so convincing, so earnest, so determined, that we actually thought he may, this time, finally deliver on his promise. He knew well enough of the problems we had endured for so long; of the times we had been unable to get to or from our house for days on end because a few hours of heavy rain had turned the access road into a quagmire. He knew because we had told him many times. Perhaps this time it would really happen.

Four weeks later, as we cleared the brow of the hill and looked down to our own little piece of Italy, we held our breath: would it be deflation or elation? We need not have wondered – the road was as bad as ever. Nothing had been done. Another Italian promise had been broken, or more likely forgotten about within minutes of our discussion. It was so often the way of things, particularly when it came to any dealings with Italian bureaucracy at even the most local level.

* * * * *

Scenario two: It had been as severe a winter in our corner of Le Marche as many locals could remember. Snow had lain for weeks. It had been over three feet deep at its worst, we were assured, and even now, well into March, the slow thaw had only reduced it by half. When we had been there at Christmas, we had been able to have breakfast and lunch outside on the terrace and enjoy warm sunshine and cloudless skies. Yet early spring had delivered blizzards of rare ferocity.

We had arrived from England that morning and had feared the worst as we approached Casa Rosa. Our brave little 4x4 had slithered its way down the hill with us tense with anxiety; would we make it through or would we slide to a halt and have to finish the icy journey by foot? We got there. The house was fine, the electricity, unusually, was still on, but the gas boiler was, as the Italians love to say, 'kaput'. So no central heating and no hot water.

We had called the boiler engineers in the full expectation that, even if we got an answer, it would be to tell us that they could not help, that they were, literally, snowed under with call-outs, that they could never get down the track to our house and, anyway, it was nearly the weekend. But we were wrong: they would send an engineer and he would be there within the hour.

It was absurd to believe them, of course. They had all the reasons they could ever need to leave us stranded. What could we do? Indoors was like being in a fridge. While heavy clothing and a couple of fan heaters may see us through, the absence of hot water was too much to bear; we would have to find a hotel.

As we looked out of the window at the arctic scene, a vision suddenly appeared on the crest of the hill. For a moment we could hardly make it out, a jerky white movement against a backdrop of snow. As it came slowly towards us, we realised it was a vehicle, bouncing from side to side down the uneven track, snow up to the top of its wheels at times. Was it a mirage, caused by snow-blindness or despair? No, it was a little white Fiat Panda van and it was coming to our rescue. It slid to a halt outside the house, a young man in an immaculate blue overall climbed out and greeted us, in a matter-of-fact way, making no reference to the extreme weather or the extraordinary odyssey he had just undertaken to reach us. Painstakingly he dismantled the reluctant boiler, whispered a few magic spells, fired it up and declared it fixed. We didn't know whether to laugh or cry. He then spent slightly longer silently hand-crafting the paperwork and invoice than he had on repairing the boiler.

To say that we thanked him profusely would be to understate it. We paid his bill, exchanged *ciao*s and off he went. He had somehow navigated his way down the hill to us but surely he would never make it back up. He did: slowly, carefully, deliberately, the Panda picked its way through the snow and finally vanished over the crown of the hill.

The mayor had delivered failure just as we were beginning to half-expect success; the heating engineer had confounded our expectations of disappointment and delivered the most extraordinary, against-the-odds triumph. They are two tales that serve perfectly to illustrate the enigma, the contradiction and the complete unfathomability of Italy. No matter how well you think you know it, you never really do.

* * * * *

Rosie and I learnt countless lessons during our twelve years as Italian property owners but the overarching one that remains with us is that *La Dolce Vita* is a mirage. It has been conjured up by film-makers and dewy-eyed novelists, and perpetuated by revenue-driven glossy magazines and wealthy ex-pats who, typically, own luxury villas in Tuscany and use their riches to insulate themselves from Italian reality.

Real Italy, as witnessed by more cost-conscious foreigners like us, and which exists in the towns and villages throughout the provinces, is a very different land. Here exists a breed of natives who may win your heart or break it, cut you dead or enfold you with the warmest of hugs; who may stare open-mouthed at you as though you are a two-headed extra-terrestrial or wave exuberantly and enthusiastically from across a crowded street. Enter a shop or café and it's 50-50 whether you'll be charmed and captivated or totally ignored. Often it is easy to think you have become suddenly invisible. Daily life for a Brit in provincial Italy is seldom the happy-go-lucky round of fun and sun and glorious food as is so often portrayed. It is the challenge of trying to fathom the logic of shop opening hours, of wild goose chases, of navigating unmarked roads that end in fields, coping with driving that flits between insane and inanimate, of writing off whole days to achieve the simplest of tasks. Worst of all, it is dealing with Italy's most debilitating, exhausting weapon: bureaucracy.

Don't rush off with the idea that I'm rubbishing the country that I have grown to know fairly well over the years. It has the ability, often when you least expect it, to fill you with tears of joy with its glorious landscapes and beaches, its history and architecture, its food and, yes, its people. There can be few other places on earth, surely, that can match Venice for sheer, romance-laden beauty, or Rome for its overwhelming sense of history.

The point, really, is simply this: Italy is a many-sided coin. Forget the fantasy of the 'sweet life'. Like all countries, it has its good and its bad, its laudable and its mad. When it's bad in Italy, it can be excruciating, infuriating, bewildering. But when it's good, it perhaps reaches closer to the stars than almost anywhere else.

Primo

At the beginning . . .

It had been a rare combination of circumstances that had sent us to Italy in September of 2001 in search of a property that would graft a new dimension on to our lives. It was the sort of alchemy that, in a different scenario, may cause a flash fire to start, a riverbank to burst or a new life form to be created. When all the elements coincide, the results can sometimes be explosive or momentous. For us, England was pushing us away as Europe beckoned and many other factors were mixed into the brew.

The idea of a house abroad had been no more than the most vaguely formed notion that had lain dormant in the back of our minds for years. But as the year 2000 staggered tired and stale to an end and its successor spluttered damply in, the UK seemed a pretty sorry place. The weather, like the puddles, had reached new depths, and great swathes of the countryside were inundated by floods. There seemed to be disasters almost daily on our overloaded roads. The petrol crisis was just behind us, while just ahead lay the Hatfield train disaster and the railway chaos that was its legacy.

The whole country seemed to be approaching gridlock, with transport systems failing, unrest and frustration all around and a heavy depression in the air unmatched since the three-day week a generation earlier. Of course, all these factors were merely unhappy coincidences of timing and most of them dried up along with the floodwater, but there was no escaping the feeling of gloom that had descended for a while like a clammy fog. Our work, too, was losing its sparkle.

The lure of the Continent, however, was by no means a retreat, fuelled solely by negative emotions. Europe's pull was considerable and it really was mainly positive energy that powered us forward. A succession of short foreign breaks whetted our appetites for more. All the signposts seemed to be pointing us in the same direction. It seemed one after another of our friends or acquaintances bought a holiday home abroad, usually in France, to give their lives a wonderful escape route.

Thoughts of buying abroad repeatedly darted unbidden into our minds when we discovered that property could be bought far more cheaply than we had realised. Our shapeless long-range plans began to gather substance following a wonderful holiday in Sicily in the summer of 2001. We returned to disappointing English weather and decided it was time to re-draw the parameters of our lives; a holiday home would be a key part of that.

Articles and advertisements drew wonderful pictures of southern France. Then the thought struck us: why go to France when we could go to Italy? France had seemed more accessible, but if we were looking at the south, so would usually need to fly there, we could just as easily fly to Italy. Now the ripples of excitement within us had become a tidal wave: yes, we could, perhaps, own a little place in Italy! Months earlier Rosie's mother had given us a guide book to Italy as a Christmas present. I had immersed myself in its pages of facts and figures, vivid descriptions, useful information and fascinating photographs. All of Italy's regions were dealt with in what seemed to be an objective and balanced way. An area called Le Marche had particularly intrigued me.

Squeezed between the Apennine mountains that run down Italy's spine, and the Adriatic Sea to the east, Le Marche (it means The Marches, or border country) is to the east of trendy Tuscany, almost halfway down Italy's 'leg'. It was described as an enchanting rural patchwork of old towns, hill country and long, sandy beaches. Yet, unlike Tuscany and its other western neighbour Umbria, Le Marche was virtually unknown and undiscovered by foreign holidaymakers. Its beauty was still raw and unspoilt and there was no English community of any size in the region. Le Marche's attractions were confirmed and strengthened one evening when we stumbled across a television show that featured the region as an appealing option for Brits in search of a place in the sun. Property prices were still inexpensive but were rising quickly.

Internet and library research uncovered much about the region. It had its share of fine Renaissance art and architecture and for good measure could throw in ski-ing or trekking across wild mountains, great fishing and some of Europe's finest beaches. It was almost tourist-free and inexpensive. There were nature reserves, spectacular limestone caves, an amazing breadth of natural flora and fauna, and landscape to match anything the continent can offer.

Le Marche's modest economy relied largely on small-scale industries, more often than not family businesses involving several generations. Shoes, clothing and furniture were among the most successful. Considering the nature of the countryside, agriculture made a surprisingly small contribution to the area's financial wellbeing because of the poor soil quality. However, the vast proportion of the land given over to vineyards was testament to the success of Le Marche's famous white wine, Verdicchio.

The more we read, the better it sounded. Cooking is traditional with its origins rooted firmly in peasant methods and local ingredients. English-style convenience food had been cold-shouldered by the Marchegiani and frozen food remained quite a novelty. It was all about high-quality fresh foods, locally produced and traditionally cooked. Natural crops such as fungi, nuts, field herbs and truffles played a big part in the locals' staple diet, yet curiously the Marchegiani ate more meat than any other Italians.

Ryanair, we discovered, had recently launched a twice-daily, low-cost route from London Stansted to Le Marche's main city, Ancona. The next Tuscany? A plethora of glossy magazine articles over the next few weeks would offer the same opinion. Perhaps we could be in on the start of something, a novelty for us, it must be said. If property values were soaring, our investment would surely be as safe as it could be. It was not that we were looking for a payback but natural sensible caution dictated that such factors should be borne in mind. We had seen and heard and read enough to convince us that we should investigate buying a holiday home in this lovely part of eastern Italy.

Every possible source of information and advice was plundered over the next few days and nights before we settled on the area that looked most appealing for us. It lay midway between the provincial capitals of Macerata and Ascoli Piceno, just over the border into the southernmost of Le Marche's administrative areas. The part close to the sizeable settlements of Fermo and Montegiorgio looked a favourite area on which to start focusing our search, situated midway between the Sibillini Mountains to the west and the Adriatic beaches to the east.

Using internet and email, both still pretty much in their infancy at the time, we found plenty of agents, both English and Italian, operating in Le Marche. Some specialised in restoration projects, others in homes that had been partly or fully revived and were ready for habitation. For all that this part of Italy presented a public image of a sleepy rural backwater, the region and its estate agents had some pretty sophisticated websites. There were pictures of grand houses standing in scores of acres and of collapsed hovels with quaint names. Most appeared to be falling to pieces but were set in spectacular countryside. Many were so inexpensive that we thought the calculator must be on the blink or else the value of the lira had suddenly taken off.

We decided to go over for a four-day journey in September. We did not have the first idea what we were looking for. We were sure that we would fall in love with Le Marche but did we want the challenge of a restoration job or something we could use right away? Did we want something as small as a holiday caravan or somewhere big enough to have friends or family out to stay with us?

We whittled down the hundreds of places that the internet showed us until we had produced a loose itinerary. By email and phone we planned liaisons with several agents over several days. Each of them would drive us around to a number of places. Then we would listen to our hearts and minds and make a decision. Simple really.

House hunting

It was not love at first sight when we arrived in Le Marche, but we were prepared for that. The land around most airports is rarely the stuff of dreams and Ancona was fairly typical in that respect. Even the hire car journey south along the coastal motorway revealed only a few tantalising glimpses of the region's charms, usually in the form of silhouettes on the horizon.

Once we had left the *autostrada* at Porto San Giorgio, however, and begun to head inland towards Montegiorgio and the Hotel San Paolo where we were booked to stay, we could quickly understand the origin of all the flattering adjectives. The countryside was staggeringly beautiful, a tapestry of colours, with vivid soaring hills, swooping valleys and medieval hilltop villages, all dozing peacefully under a warm September sun. We were already smitten.

The car journey from our Wiltshire home to Stansted along motorways peppered with roadworks and accidents was the longest and most gruelling leg of the entire odyssey from English village to eastern Italian town. The flight took a whisker under two hours and the sixty-mile drive from Ancona airport to Montegiorgio would have been quicker had we held the road maps the right way up. The hotel was comfortable and friendly and, as we ate splendidly and inexpensively in its dining room that night, we had difficulty containing our excitement as we reviewed our packed diary of appointments over the next three days.

Sandro had arranged to arrive at the hotel sharp at nine and got there at the Italian equivalent, a quarter past. He was to be our guide for Thursday morning. Sandro was in his late 50s, quite seriously overweight, slightly perspiring and with thinning hair. He had two mobile phones, which seemed to take it in turns to ring. He had designer sunglasses and he drove, effortlessly and expertly, with one hand, using the other one to talk with, as Italians do.

Sandro spoke not a word of English while our grasp of Italian stretched little further than a pizza menu, so our meeting in the hotel foyer was a muddled and slightly self-conscious one. He beckoned to us to sit, got out his newspaper and proceeded to read it. Then Gina arrived. Sandro's usual interpreter had been double-booked so Gina had stepped in to help, she explained in barely intelligible English. It may be a little difficult, she said, because she knew nothing about buying or selling houses and her English, never good, was now very rusty. At any event, she could not understand a single word that we said to her and we could barely make out one word in twenty that she addressed to us. It promised to be an interesting morning.

Rosie and I settled ourselves into the back of Sandro's car and set off at breakneck speed on the first of three days of glorious Le Marche sightseeing. So many times we would nudge each other to look, open-mouthed, at some impossibly beautiful expanse of scenery, or some bizarre example of Italian life. The rich canvas of the countryside was so perfect everywhere we looked. The villages, loaded with history, were invariably full of charm. The people were friendly everywhere we went. When we stopped for refreshment, the food was fresh, local and ridiculously inexpensive.

Our first destination on that first sun-drenched morning was a derelict house set in the middle of a vast field that, weeks earlier, had been a bright yellow blaze of sunflowers, but was now just stalks. It was near the little town of Monterinaldo and the panoramic setting of the house was enhanced by the fruit trees that lined the approach road. There were peach trees here and there among vines groaning under the weight of ripe grapes. The house itself looked in a desperate state. There was a jagged crack down one wall wide enough to push an arm through, except that we were unable to get close enough even to try because of the thick blanket of vegetation all around it. Restoration? It looked more like a demolition job to our untrained eyes, but the location was amazing and the asking price only around £25,000.

The next stop was a brief one, close to the larger town of Montegiorgio. The house was bigger and in slightly better condition than the previous one, but its location did not compare and, at £47,000, it was nearly double the price. Once again we could not get close enough for a good poke around because of debris and vegetation, and we knew immediately not to waste too much time there.

We had quickly realised that in this part of Italy, at least, vendors make no attempt whatsoever to smarten up their properties when they put them on the market. To leave all access possibilities blocked because they had allowed nettles and bushes to grow as they pleased was hardly likely to enhance their appeal. We lost count of the number of houses we visited but at none had anybody so much as put a broom round or even made the most cursory effort to tidy up. At one hovel, the entire floor of the main bedroom was covered with potatoes. At another we found dead scorpions in the kitchen sink. Several had just abandoned ancient sticks of furniture to rot. It does not exactly boost a house's prospects of persuading an eager buyer to part with his hard-earned lire, yet for some reason, presentation skills do not appear to be in the Italian psyche. It did not seem to fit well with a nation normally so obsessed with *la bella figura*.

Third on our itinerary that morning was a large peach-rendered farmhouse sitting unobtrusively in the most stunning location alongside a gently curving track high on a ridge a mile or two out of Montegiorgio. While not a building of great beauty, it was well proportioned, several hundred yards from any neighbours and offered incredible views for miles in every direction. There were fields of every hue stretching to the horizon, speckled here and there with cottages and small villages. In the far distance to the west we could discern the blue-grey silhouette of the Sibillini Mountains, to the east the faint shimmer of the sun bouncing off the Adriatic.

The peach-rendered house near Montegiorgio: great location but too big for us?

The house was unoccupied and was being marketed as a restoration project. The asking price was £50,000, which seemed, to us, very reasonable. It looked sound and solidly constructed and for once we were able to go inside and have a proper look around. All the living rooms were upstairs, as is the tradition for farmhouses and cottages in this area; downstairs would have belonged to the animals. The ground-floor chambers were roomy and light and would undoubtedly have made wonderful living accommodation. Access to the upstairs was via an outside concrete staircase. Tucked away some yards from the main house, its back hard against the roadside verge, was an outbuilding the size of a generous double garage. It had probably been used as a workshop and machinery store and would have been quite large enough to convert into a self-contained bedsit.

The place was lovely and we were much taken with it. Ideas sped through our minds. Maybe it was too big for a holiday home. Would its proportions make the restoration cost prohibitively high? Back home in rural Wiltshire, such a house, even in that condition, would have cost maybe six times as much. We were much taken with the peach-coloured house and may well buy it. But then what? We were covered in confusion.

The last venue of our morning with Sandro and Gina was near the village of Fermano, where they showed us a lovely white-painted house, allegedly in excellent condition inside. However, they had no key so we could not see for ourselves. It was a most attractive place and, at £56,000, seemed a lot of house for a reasonable price. But it was alongside a fairly busy road. It occurred to us, too, that one of Le Marche's greatest assets was its staggeringly beautiful countryside and if you lived in a house where you could not see it, you may as well be in some nondescript suburb. A nice house but not for us, we agreed.

Sandro had his afternoon arranged elsewhere and we, too, had other plans so we bade farewell to our hosts and arranged to see them again the next morning to visit some more houses. We drove west towards the mountains and the little town of Amandola. We had set up our liaison with agents Michael and Debbie by email and phone and met up with them at an outside table of *Bar Belli* just off the main square. They were business partners, both English. We hit it off quickly with them both and were certainly glad to be able to communicate again without resorting to sign language.

There was a common theme to the succession of houses they drove us around on that hot Thursday afternoon: they were all hovels. Some were in worse order than others but without exception they were in a sad state of disrepair. It was rather like visiting the sick.

Near Comunanza we saw a desperately dilapidated farmhouse, with a small cottage in its overgrown grounds. They were both in need of a complete rebuild and were a snip at £16,000. A rebuild involves careful demolition, saving and re-using as many of the original materials as possible, and starting afresh, having first negotiated a way through the Italian planning process. The costs would have been astronomical, although the final result would have been wonderful. An enormously grand house in some godforsaken hamlet was ours for only £18,000 but it was just too big a job and actually a bit scary. The other places we were shown were not quite that bad but all fell a long way short of our hopes. On the journey back to Amandola, we stopped at the tiny hamlet of San Ippolito for Michael to show us his own home. Nearby stood a pair of semi-detached cottages that he and Debbie were keen for us to see. The one on the left was uninhabited and in a desperate state of disrepair but the other had been fully renovated. It was small but pretty and had beautiful views of the mountains and landscape. The owner, Alfredo, was happy to show us around.

He was a wealthy Roman businessman who had bought the cottage as a holiday escape but his wife hated it with a passion and he had been forced to choose between his dream of a rural retreat and his marriage. There seemed to have been considerable reluctance and heart-searching before he had reached his verdict but the house was now for sale. For the cottage, in perfect condition, and all its furniture, fixtures and fittings, Alfredo was looking for about £75,000. It was small, with one spacious living room, a well-planned little kitchen and two bedrooms.

Alfredo's house: small but perfectly formed. An instant solution?

We were impressed but was this what we wanted? Did we want semi-detached, especially when the other half looked as though it may fall down at any moment? It was apparently going to be renovated but who could say when it would be done or what impact the work would have on Alfredo's house? On the other hand, this was an instant solution, totally up-together, even furnished. There would not be another lira to spend. Yes, we shall probably buy Alfredo's house. Or the Peach House? No, Alfredo's it would be. Almost certainly. Next morning with Sandro and Gina proved fruitless and disappointing, though our sightseeing tour of Le Marche from the back seat was most enjoyable. We looked at a couple of houses which we did not like. A sprawling ruin near Monterinaldo was in reasonable condition but its price tag of £56,500 was a deterrent in view of the repair bills. Another, close to Macerata, was huge and would have set us back £69,000.

There was no time for lunch as we had to head back west to Amandola in time for our appointment with another agent, Stefano. His estate agency role was merely a sideline to his main business running a shop in the town, specialising in kitchen and bathroom fittings and various other ironmongery hardware. He showed us a homespun scrapbook of properties he had for sale. It was like catalogue shopping.

There was only one that caught our eye, a small place close to the little town of Gualdo. We had already decided to buy the Peach House, of course, or was it Alfredo's place? But we had pre-arranged our meeting Stefano so we ought to make the effort to generate or at least feign some interest in one of his houses.

Casa Linda was situated down a long narrow lane, through trees. It was a fairly typical small cottage but fully restored, totally up-together, and was only £46,000. It had the characteristic outside staircase, but inside stairs had also been installed and the place was in excellent order. There was a reasonable chunk of land with it, although probably half comprised dense scrubby trees. The views left much to be desired because of the vegetation and the lie of the land but, in one direction at least, you could see something of the beauty of the landscape.

Casa Linda: amazing value, but doubts.

There were a couple of minor niggles, though. The place was in shade, and although that was largely due to the time of the day and the angle of sun, it had the look somehow of a place that did not see too much sun. Also there was a fairly steep grass bank quite close to one side, beyond which was the wall of a large modernised house. Stefano assured us it belonged to a family of Germans who were rarely there, and their presence would in no way impinge on our privacy. Finally there was condensation evident on the upstairs windows. Well, after all, the place has been closed and unused for some time, we thought. But then again this was late summer. But the price. And the value for money.

It was not exactly your Italian dream cottage in the sun but it was a fully refurbished traditional cottage at a bargain price. Yes, that was it. Forget the Peach House, never mind Alfredo's. This little place near Gualdo had won the day. We gushed excitedly at Stefano that we almost certainly wanted to buy it. He said we should make contact with his head office and he would await developments. So that was it then for us, a successful conclusion. It would definitely be Casa Linda. Probably.

Journey's end

Our conversation over dinner in the hotel that night veered between the same two topics that had dominated most of our meals in Le Marche: the wonderful freshness and taste of the food and wine we were enjoying and the extraordinary houses that we had seen that day. Each evening, of course, we seemed to be enthusing about the latest one that we had chosen to buy and this time it was the turn of the little house at Gualdo. Our meal was disturbed this time, however, when Anna, the agent we had arranged to meet the following morning for our final series of appointments, phoned us to return our attempts to call her earlier. We told her that we had found the place we had decided to buy. All hers, we knew, had been renovation projects and we told her that, after our in-depth research of the options, we found the idea of a place where all the work had been done most appealing. Perhaps we should save her time and ours and just forget tomorrow, we suggested.

Anna understood but, having listened to our thoughts, felt it would still be worthwhile meeting up the next day. She had a couple of places to show us and was sure we would be interested. With some reluctance and considerable weariness, we agreed. We really had trailed around quite enough Italian ruins and hopeless heaps of brick dust and debris but we would honour the arrangement and see what Anna had to show us. She said she would collect us at half past nine next morning – 'that's an Italian half nine,' she added. We understood.

She arrived a little after ten and told us what she had on our agenda. Rosie and I exchanged disappointed glances when she told us none of the properties was refurbished and habitable. But the die was cast and we had nothing to lose, other than a few uncommitted hours.

She drove us first to a beautiful large farmhouse only a few minutes from Montegiorgio. It was a fine old building, rendered in a soft peach colour at the front and displaying its original stone structure at the rear. It had, by the look of it, been extended more than once and was set in plenty of land in a nice elevated position. But it was far bigger than we could possibly have use for unless we were going into the bed-and-breakfast business. We were again unable to get in as Anna had forgotten the key. It really mattered little because it would not have suited us whatever the interior was like. But it was a very splendid house, one of the nicest we had seen.

Second on her list was a sandstone farmhouse at Penna San Giovanni. It was rather curiously situated, far too close to a neighbour's yapping dogs, and somehow contrived to be far smaller on its three floors inside than it appeared from the outside. Had we seen it as the first viewing on our first morning we may have been impressed. Now we were veterans at this viewing business and we could barely offer it a second glance. Anyway we were buying Casa Linda.

The house that Anna had most wanted us to see was the one she had kept until last. Until yesterday it was going to be bought by an English couple who had fallen in love with its amazing location, she explained, but they had suddenly phoned to say the deal was off. They gave no reason for their sudden U-turn but Anna sensed that a pretty seismic marital disagreement was at the root of it.

So the little old farmhouse, a mile outside the hilltop village of Montottone, was suddenly available again. Although it did not fit our criteria in that it was a restoration project, Anna was certain that we would love it. Oh dear, Rosie and I felt. The last place on the last day and it will not be what we want. Thank goodness we had Casa Linda tucked safely in our back pocket.

We turned off the road on the village outskirts and up a narrow rutted 'white road', as they are known. Then a left into another and suddenly we found ourselves driving gently downhill along the narrow spine of a high ridge. To left and right you could see forever. Ahead we could see that the narrow sun-washed lane twisted steeply down into the distance, the route punctuated by the presence of two old houses. The furthest of them was our destination.

But first, to reach it, Anna had to park her car in the road as it was impassable, too difficult even for her sturdy estate car to negotiate. We walked the rest of the way, soothed by her assurance that the road would be made good as soon as a house sale went through.

The little house sat there quietly in the mid-afternoon sun, like a modest jewel set in the most breathtaking landscape.

Fanciful, perhaps, but it reminded me of a lonely child waiting to be embraced. We both knew in an instant that this was the rainbow's end for us.

The eastern end that faced us as we approached featured three narrow windows on the ground floor, the animal quarters. Upstairs there was a full-sized window to the right and the filled-in ghost of a window to the left. The left-hand side of the little house looked out across a sweep of meadow, which belonged to the property and sloped sharply down away from it. There were the traditional outside steps leading up to the doors into what would have been the living quarters above. Either side of the door was a window. Below was a wide door, beneath the steps, into the right-hand stable area; beside it another into the left-hand section.

Attached to the rear of the house were two separate lean-tos in the same honey-coloured old brick, one containing a beautifully crafted old pizza oven, as precise as a wasps' nest, the other, lower, one being a pig sty. In that direction, to the west, lay a vineyard, its vines groaning under the weight of the ripe grapes, its nearest rows only feet from the building. The first seven or eight rows, maybe eight vines across, went with the house, we were told. The farmer would tend them and harvest them with his own and pay us an annual rent in the most agreeable currency of a few bottles of wine.

Way beyond the vineyard, as little more than faint suggestions on the distant horizon, we could pick out the unmistakable grey shape of the Sibillini Mountains. Sloping sharply down from the right-hand northern side of the house was an olive grove, the silver foliage of the trees shining in the sun as if frosted. Only the first line of three trees came with the house. Beyond them ran a track that led through to the vineyard and was only ever used by the tractor driver.

In every direction the landscape was stunning. The only sound we could hear was birdsong spilling from the trees around the little stream which ran along the foot of the hill just beyond the meadow. The scene was so characteristic Le Marche, so absolutely soul-enriching and beautiful, that probably nothing could have blocked our instantly formed plan to own this little house.

Like a conjuror pulling a rabbit from a hat, Anna amazed us by producing a set of heavy old keys so we would be able to look inside. We were not expecting much and we did not get much. It was in a dire state. In the downstairs animal quarters, both rooms were almost impenetrable because of the long whippy brambles that had encroached, as well as a strange collection of odds and ends that had probably once belonged to items of farm machinery or crude furniture. In one of the chambers, one full wall incorporated concrete feeding troughs for the animals that had been its last occupants – or at least its last official ones. Lizards scurried here and there and no doubt they had other uninvited companions. The floors were filthy and coated in dirt but a light scrape of the foot revealed traditional terracotta tiling right through. Across the ceiling were massive support beams of chestnut, painted white and peppered with worm holes.

We entered the upper floor via the outside steps and the double doors at their summit. Here the squatters were more obvious and certainly more numerous. Two of the four rooms were infested with bats, some flying jerkily and sleepily from berth to berth but most, probably dozens of them, attached to the ceilings.

The four rooms were all roughly the same size, around four metres square, and all had shuttered windows so were in darkness as we entered. Once the shutters were thrown back, the daylight flooded in, illuminating half a ton of bat droppings, more old bits of what had once probably been furniture, and a collection of demijohns and various wine casks. Of far more interest, though, were the views out of the windows, which in every direction were simply astonishing. The tiled floors upstairs looked to be in poor condition and in one room, most had collapsed, leaving a gaping hole through into the room below.

Anna had arranged for the house's owner, Maria-Francesca, to meet us there. She arrived a few minutes later, greeted us warmly and revealed that the house had belonged to her grandfather and then her father, who had bequeathed it to her on his recent death. It had last been modernised in the 1930s and last lived in maybe thirty years ago.

Its official designation was 'SN' – *senza numero*, without number. The family, she confided, had always called it *La Pisciarella*, or 'little pee', referring with some sort of Italian humour we had not yet fathomed to the little stream beyond the trees at the foot of the sloping meadow. The asking price for the house and its acre of land was the lira equivalent of £26,000.

When we finally managed to drag ourselves away from the house, we told Anna that we now understood why she had so wanted us to see it. We had set our hearts on a ready-made Italian bolthole but the little house had completely changed our minds. We told her of the Gualdo house and she knew of it, describing it exactly. It was a botched job, she said, damaged by the earthquake that had struck Assisi in neighbouring Umbria a few years earlier, and shoddily patched up. Those in the property business knew it, which was why it had not sold. It was damp and had serious structural concerns. We believed her and were mighty relieved to know it.

We drove into the village of Montottone and walked, almost proprietorially, around its narrow streets. We were utterly captivated by its cobbled streets and its peaceful demeanour as it sat on its hilltop perch in the sunshine. We were absolutely sure that we would get to know this little place well and that this would turn out to be a landmark day for us.

We returned to our hotel with Anna and sat at an outside table in the early evening sunshine, taking detailed notes as she talked us through the maze of Italian red tape that lay ahead. We were prepared for the long haul and happy that she would be our agent. We were excited about the house which by now we had christened, at least in our own minds, Casa Rosa. We had spotted a beautiful crimson rose growing near the front door and our home in Wiltshire happened to be called Rose Cottage.

The rose that gave Casa Rosa its name.

Anna explained that, in Italy, a verbal agreement on a house sale was as rock-solid as a written one. If we made an offer and the owner accepted it, the deal was sealed. There would be no going back, no gazumping. That suited us. Contracts would soon be drawn up, at which time we would hand over a deposit. After a couple of months, both parties would complete the transaction with a small ceremony in the offices of the public *notaio* when the balance would be paid over.

Meanwhile Anna would find a *geometra*, a surveyor/architect, who would be the conduit in order to get plans drawn up and obtain the necessary planning permission, and builders to carry out the restoration work at the house. She had done this sort of work for many years and had a reliable list of contacts whose work she could trust. Having paced out the dimensions of the house, she reckoned the restoration cost would be around £32,000 as it was a straightforward and accessible site. With the fees for Anna and the *geometra*, various taxes and other costs such as charges for connection of services, we reckoned the bottom line for buying and repairing our lovely little house should be around £65,000. It would still have to be furnished but that was far less than Alfredo's place, for instance, and his was semi-detached. The Little Pee was the one for us.

It was September. Purchase could be completed before Christmas, the builders on site by March and, with a following wind, Casa Rosa could be ready for occupation by June or July of 2002. It seemed a long time to have to wait when we could have had six months' use of Alfredo's place by then but it would be worth it.

We flew back to England the next day, emailed an offer of the asking price and the following day heard that it had been accepted and the little house on the hillside was going to be ours. The date was that fateful day that has become known throughout the world as 'nine eleven': September 11, 2001. That terrible day that brought death to thousands and shock to millions, when the Twin Towers of New York were attacked, was the day our lives changed too.

The end of the rainbow: Casa Rosa, on the day of our first visit in September 2001.

A change of plan

Our Italian secret brought us comfort and excitement as another damp and gloomy autumn enveloped us, and all the factors that had pointed us towards buying a house abroad were present with a vengeance. It was then that we took the decision to quit our jobs, sell up and move lock, stock and barrel to Italy.

As the weeks had passed since our visit to Le Marche, our little house had shrunk in our minds. We had photographs to help prompt our memories, but although it was easy enough to recall its appearance and surroundings, it was harder to be clear about its dimensions. Yet so determined were we to make the pieces fit that we convinced ourselves we could cope. This was going to be a great watershed in our lives and we should use it as a chance to make a fresh beginning.

Then there were the financial aspects. Walking boldly away from stressful jobs was one thing, walking away from the salaries that went with them was quite another. There followed many hours with a calculator, trying desperately to balance soft-hearted emotions with hard-headed sense.

A dozen schemes and their innumerable variations raced through our minds and discussions as we strove to conjure a mental picture of the lifestyle we wanted to immerse ourselves in for the next phase of our lives. With property so cheap and plentiful in Le Marche, perhaps we could buy two or three small houses, renovate one or two per year and sell them on to provide ourselves with an ongoing income. There was a moral dimension here that troubled us but surely, we argued, it was better for the region that its old farmhouses were revived rather than allowed to collapse, even if the motive was mainly pecuniary. Alternatively we could modernise them and let them as holiday homes, which would still produce an income, maintain assets that would appreciate and provide our lives with a work focus. Should Casa Rosa prove too small for a permanent home, we could let it and move into a bigger one. The permutations were endless.

The safety net was always there, too. If things did not work out for us, or we found that the Italian way of life lost its appeal once we were swallowed up by it, then we could always sell up, come back and resume our English lives. When all was said and done, it was no sort of gamble at all, really, just a unique opportunity for a middle-aged adventure. The decision taken, we set about constructing a sort of business plan, pulling together all the financial strands. Then we devised our timetable towards freedom. We were due to complete the purchase of Casa Rosa in December, the builders would move on site in March and it would be finished by July. Translate all those dates into Italian so add on a couple of months to get closer to reality.

Numerous details still plagued us, such as how to move our belongings and whether to take a car or buy one in Italy. These things, we were sure, would start to fall into place as time moved on.

Inside the ground floor of the house before the start of the renovation.

The legal process

We had read and heard many stories about Italy's singular approach to officialdom. The Italians have developed an enviable expertise when it comes to dodging their financial responsibilities. Diddling the taxman or the planner is regarded, not as an antisocial or, heaven forbid, unlawful act, but a duty, a national pastime, even a sport.

Whole industries have grown up and thrived, specialising in guiding the average Italian through the minefield of legislation, safely reaching the other end having satisfied the sometimes preposterous demands of authority while keeping as many of their cash as possible snugly in their pockets.

Such practised skill is enviable, if confusing, all the more so since so much of this large-scale evasion of responsibility seems to be accepted by the state in all its many forms. We knew this long before we returned to Le Marche for a few bitter cold days just before Christmas, but an hour or two in the public *notaio*'s offices high on a hill in Fermo taught us more about the unique Italian mentality than any written words. We were there to formally complete the purchase of Casa Rosa, an exciting landmark day for us. Soon we would own a tiny speck on the great map of Italy.

The *notaio* is the state's representative at the ceremony, responsible to neither side but there to ensure fair play and complete the numerous formalities. We had been thoroughly prepared in advance by Anna, who was experienced in such matters but who still seemed slightly embarrassed and amused by the whole affair.

We had been told to bring pre-drawn cheques in order to pay the *notaio*'s fees and costs, and to pay the vendor a notional sum for the house. Notional means the figure that all parties – buyers, sellers and *notaio* – agree upon as being the least they can get away with declaring officially. It bore little relation to the price actually agreed between buyer and seller because to declare the true figure would mean paying tax on it. A lower price means a lower tax charge.

The official purchase price of Casa Rosa had been fixed at around £16,000. The other £10,000, in bundles of lire squeezed into a large brown envelope, was handed by us to Anna and thence to the vendor after the *notaio* had made an extravagant show of announcing that he was leaving the room for a few minutes to have a cigarette. By the time he returned, the deal was done. (These were the dying days of the Italian lira; a few weeks later, in January 2002, it vanished and the euro took its place. Many Italians would swear that prices doubled overnight). Three years later, we would go through a similar charade at a *nataio*'s office when we bought a further seven acres of land surrounding Casa Rosa from Maria-Francesca. It comprised a large field to the south, another to the north, as well as the whole of the vineyard to the west, and the olive orchard.

The legalities completed and the deal sealed and celebrated with a glass of wine in a packed bar nearby, Rosie and I headed back to Montottone with Anna to renew acquaintances with the little house that we now owned. The December landscape was raw and bleak compared with its appearance the last time we had been there. Even in its winter clothes it was impressive, although the dominant colour now was brown in its many shades rather than the greens that had held sway before. Our sumptuous vines were now drab skeletons, their summer foliage and fruit now stripped away. The olive trees seemed desperately out of place.

The house looked sad and cold but we were delighted to note that it was larger than we had remembered. We spent some time inside, out of the wind, and viewed its rooms with our minds full of thoughts of how it could mould to our lives, and vice versa. The place was a mess of the sort of odd detritus that somehow builds up in abandoned houses surrounded by nature. After renovation, although it would still be small, it should be more than adequate for our needs.

We had a little spare time to look at some of the countryside and also had the opportunity to examine some of the work carried out by the builders Anna was planning to employ to work on our house. We saw a tiny house built awkwardly into the side of a steep verge. It was three-quarters of the way through renovation, and the builders were obviously doing a beautiful job. Then we travelled a few miles to inspect a project they had carried out some months earlier, converting a big tumbledown water mill into luxurious living accommodation. Its conversion was breathtaking in conception and the workmanship was outstanding, a blend of sensitivity and imagination that delighted us.

The two Fabios and a labourer at work on the interior of the house.

Doubts and dithering

It is hard to say precisely when the doubts began to creep into our minds but it was some time between our December 2001 visit to complete the purchase of the house and our return to Le Marche the following April. Nor can I recall with any great clarity what triggered our worries. With hindsight, however, it would have been strange had we found ourselves able to drive forward such a life-changing adventure without a mental wobble or two on the way.

We were still infected with the Italy bug, of course. The romantic storyline of our planned big picture remained as appealing as ever, especially the final scene, visualised through soft-focus lens, of the two of us sipping wine on our peaceful terrace, gazing wistfully at distant peaks and planning our next drive to Bologna or ferry trip to the Greek islands. It was getting to that appealing scene that most troubled us, the sheer terrifying logistics of it all.

The concerns ranged from the mundane – if we take all our books with us, there would be no room for furniture, but if we put them in store, they might deteriorate – to the fundamental: what if we found after only a couple of weeks that we simply hated it? Moving countries is a bit like turning round an oil tanker: it takes time.

Then there was the red tape jungle, nowhere more dense than in Italy. The more we delved, the more complicated it all seemed and new laws seemed to be enacted every day. The prospect of escaping from the grinding routine of our present lives was attractive but what if we found that an unstructured, unhurried approach was tedious and soul-destroying? And after years, as journalists, of instinctively challenging authority in all its forms, would we be able to bend the knee to every self-important Italian jobsworth?

One strand of our latest masterplan had been to buy a small flat in England to provide us with a letting income and, if necessary, a bolthole should panic set in and the need for a swift return become overwhelming. Now, suddenly, the price of flats had soared, the buy-to-let boom had tailed off and the whole business of employing an agent, dealing with leases and so on seemed too fraught with complications.

We were still sure that we wanted more of the Italian adventure and felt great warmth and affection for Casa Rosa and its glorious hillside setting. But selling up, turning our backs on our homeland and moving lock, stock and barrel to a remote corner of southern Europe now seemed too much like leaping off a cliff.

Our thought processes now took many more twists and turns before we settled on the formula that felt right. We would strike a balance: sell our English home as planned and buy a small house in England. It would be our home base, providing the psychological and bureaucratic anchor that we needed. We could then divide our time as we liked between England and Italy, the best of both worlds. It seemed the perfect recipe.

Delight and delay

In April of 2002 it was time to visit Le Marche again to get more wheels turning. The weather was disappointingly cool and occasionally damp, but we were assured that February and March had been lovely. Nature now seemed to promise much for the months ahead, but the temperatures dipped sharply by evening.

As on our last visit, we had opted again to stay at the little *pensione* in Montottone, and our kind hosts, Lorella and Oreste, were generous with their time and advice as we took our early solo steps through the jungle of Italian bureaucracy. They steered us through a couple of potentially difficult transactions in Fermo. First, Lorella accompanied us to the tax office so that we could obtain our *codice fiscale*, a sort of Italian national insurance registration that is the passport to so many things in Italy. Then Oreste came with us to the mobile phone shop and with his help, we succeeded in buying an Italian SIM card that we could use in our mobile each time we visited the country.

We had already set up a temporary account with a local branch of Banca delle Marche and, after withdrawing heaps of cash, now in euros, we met Anna as arranged, and handed it to her so that she could start paying the builders. We were joined at lunch by Vincenzo, our *geometra*, who would be dealing with the planning details and liaising on our behalf with the builders and the local authority.

He said he liked our house and felt the renovation work would be uncomplicated. The not-so-good news, said Anna, was that the builders, originally expected to start work in March, would not now be on site until June because of unforeseen delays encountered on a previous job. This, we came to realise, would not only become the shape of things to come but was completely the norm when it came to Italian builders.

After lunch we drove to Casa Rosa where we were to be joined by the two men who were to carry out the work. The builders were both called Fabio. Anna had used them often before and vouched for their reliability and workmanship, examples of which we had seen first-hand during our December visit.

Our disappointment at the latest delay in the start of work was balanced by our mounting excitement, having at last met the Fabios and discussed, for the first time, the details of what would be done. The technical aspect of the work, such as floor and roof repairs and wall reinforcement, would be dealt with by Vincenzo and the Fabios. We could now thrash out the broad outline of the renovation.

Upstairs two of the four small rooms would be converted into one large master bedroom. It would have views in three directions and be spacious enough to accommodate writing desks and computers. Another of the original small rooms would have a chunk sliced off to take an internal staircase and landing, and the rest of it would be converted into a bathroom. The fourth little room would be our guest bedroom.

On the ground floor, the two stables would be knocked through into one big room, but the dividing wall was load-bearing so would have to be heavily reinforced. The two chambers would be unified by virtue of two archways, which ought to look attractive and provide a division between sitting and eating areas. At the rear of the house, the old pizza oven would, sadly, have to be demolished, as would the pigsty. In their place would be built a kitchen, which would look out on to the vineyard and distant mountains.

Local authority planners in Italy tend to be sensitive about any new development, a stance that is to be applauded because once an area of beautiful landscape is scarred by ugly buildings or inappropriate work, it can stand as a mocking embarrassment for years. Massive enlargement of small homes, such as had become prevalent in rural England, for example, was forbidden in Le Marche. New building was usually limited to the dimensions of the old building it was replacing, although these rules have been relaxed in recent years. A kitchen the size of the combined area of the existing pigsty and oven would be fine, we felt.

That same new-for-old formula could, we hoped, work to our advantage in due course. We had noticed that, near the entrance to our land, there were the brick ruins of what had probably once been a store of some kind. It was almost completely collapsed and engulfed by brambles, shrubs and grasses that had opportunistically colonised the site. But the ground area it occupied was about the size of a large garage and would make perfect studio-type guest quarters or *casetta*, large enough for a double bedroom and shower room.

Anna and the Fabios could see no great snags with the plan and would discuss it with Vincenzo. The *casetta*, should it happen, would probably come later, depending on costs, work progress and our constantly changing plans of how to use the house. Into the same category we placed the idea of a modest swimming pool. The site was private enough, and if a pool could be built discreetly, its presence would hugely boost any potential letting income, Anna assured us.

Our business now over, we used our last full day to have a further look at Le Marche in the spring time. Our unhurried drive through the countryside revealed scenes and sights that we had not noticed previously but went to confirm for us the year-round beauty of this special region. We drove, across country, to the coast and the seaside resort, San Benedetto del Tronto. The beautiful sandy beach was virtually deserted even on this fine, warm April day.

We were delighted, too, to have renewed acquaintance with Montottone. Sara, the friendly woman running the village shop, greeted us warmly, obviously remembering our clumsy attempts at communication last time. It was a splendid little shop that seemed to stock everything, and the fruit and vegetables, fresh every day and limited to varieties in season, were marvellous.

Montottone was also fortunate indeed to have in its small midst a most excellent restaurant. We had discovered it in December, when we had eaten lunch and supper there most days, and did so again on this trip. Like most small Le Marche businesses, *La Brocca* was a family-run venture, with a restaurant and adjoining bar. The village also boasted a twice-monthly street market. The little square is laid out with a dozen or so stalls, offering such wares as fish, cheeses, clothing, shoes, tools and plants.

It had been another enjoyable flirtation with Le Marche and again we were sad to be leaving so soon. Our big plan had moved on another step or two but with a willingness to rethink or adapt to changing circumstances. Having decided to buy a permanent house in England, we felt more confident that we could cope with life in Italy. We would probably spend most of the year in England, with a few spells, of several weeks each, in Casa Rosa. When we were not there, we could let it as a holiday place.

Too many people had used the word 'brave' when we had told them of our original plans but this felt safer. Maybe one day we would end up settling permanently in Le Marche, or using it, as we had first intended, as our launch pad to see the world. Time would tell. You cannot properly predict emotions until you reach them.

Work in progress.

A dash with cash

Any stabs of pain we had felt about leaving the Wiltshire cottage that had been our home for seven years were overcome when we found exactly the sort of home we needed, 25 miles away in Dorset. It was a smallish Victorian warehouse, gutted and imaginatively transformed into modern living accommodation. It was smack in the middle of town but if we pined for the taste of rural tranquillity, we could gorge ourselves on it during our stays in Le Marche.

We had not intended to return to Italy until late summer to check on the builders' progress and maybe to start looking for some basic items of furniture for the house. But our carefully formulated plans to enable Anna, our agent, to access the funds that we would drip-feed into our Italian bank account did not work. She had not wanted cash or cheques to go through her bank account as this would have attracted tax liabilities. Perish the thought. The idea had been that we would draw cheques, made out to cash, which she could then present at our bank branch and walk off with euros.

Either our helpful bank manager misled us, or we misinterpreted his words or, most likely, the rules changed yet again, but suddenly it could not be done without Anna having to account for the destination of the cash and thus incurring an unmerited tax demand. All other options explored, we decided that we would have to fly out again, withdraw the cash ourselves and hand it over to her.

Our June flight from Stansted to Ancona was delayed by several hours. There was an air traffic control dispute affecting France and various other bits of western Europe and that very afternoon Italy had been eliminated from the World Cup by South Korea, which had thrown the Italian nation into mourning. The reason for our three additional hours in Stansted's lounges, however, was at first airily announced as being 'technical problems'. Subsequently it transpired that our plane had had to be sent on a search-and-rescue mission when the engine of another Ryanair craft refused to spark into life on some remote Irish airfield. We got to Lorella's *pensione* in Montottone at two in the morning, having phoned from the tarmac at Stansted to warn her; she had left a key under the mat.

We awoke next morning to a glorious summer's day. It was beautifully warm from early morning until late in the evening but the night-time temperature was pleasantly cool and sleep came easily. We had now seen Le Marche in all seasons of the year. It had a unique beauty in all of them but summer seemed to suit it best.

First on our agenda was a trip to Casa Rosa. The builders had actually done a couple of weeks' work before Vincenzo, the *geometra*, had told them to stop because of a hitch with the local planning office. In Italy, much depends on the officiousness or otherwise of the be-suited ones at the local councils. Ours was a young man rapidly gaining a certain notoriety, it seemed. He and our man Vincenzo had evidently exchanged a good deal of arm waving and pointing until it was agreed that new additional permissions had to be sought and yet more paperwork generated. The planner, it transpired, knew our house well so he also knew that Vincenzo had been slightly economical with the truth. The proposed change of use of the ground floor from stabling to living seemed to be the nub of the problem, as far as we could grasp. So the Fabios had been ordered to down tools.

Our little house looked distinctly sad, like the victim of a mugging. The shroud of dense ivy had been stripped from the roof and walls. Rotten windows had been removed. The pizza oven and pigsty at the back had been demolished and a concrete base laid in readiness for the new kitchen, making the house seem smaller than ever. All the digging out had been done for the drains and septic tank. The old wine demijohns that had been sitting under cobwebs and bat droppings in the house had been removed and lined up out of harm's way.

But if the house itself looked battered and bruised, the countryside all around it was sensational. Summer was in its fruitful prime. The vines were weighed down with fat clusters of half-grown fruits. The olive trees shone silver-white in the sun. An adjoining field which, in April, had been full of little shoots, was now, as if in a glorious painting, a blaze of golden yellow sunflowers, in serried ranks like a million toy soldiers. Our little sloping meadow had a haze of heat over it and the grass was now chest high, moving gently in the whispers of warm air. Close to the house, lizards scuttled everywhere and there were flowers we had never known were there – poppies the colour of new blood, delicate mauve geraniums and tiny white stitchwort, all adding to the dazzling tapestry.

We were thrilled to see that, amid all the earth-moving turmoil that the bulldozer had wreaked as it dug out drain runs and footings, our rose had somehow survived. Some unwelcome invaders had been grubbed out, though, including a vast clump of bamboo. Le Marche's endemic flora is protected and the Fabios had had to promise the local authority that they would honour that most worthy agreement.

The scenario was everything we had dreamt that it could be and so much more. If we could not yet quite visualise ourselves sitting on the terrace, glass in hand, watching a red Italian sun vanish slowly behind the distant Sibillini Mountains, at least the weather was more in keeping now and the whole business seemed that little bit more attainable.

We dealt with the bank business which had necessitated our unscheduled visit and handed another pile of cash to Anna. On our arrival in the early hours, we had observed that much of the little square outside the *pensione* was covered with staging that had obviously been used for some sort of performance. It turned out to have been Montottone's annual gnocchi festival. We were disappointed to have missed it.

With only two days at our disposal on this trip, there was little time for exploring but we did drive to Amandola that evening for a most memorable pizza. Next day, before setting off for the airport, we had time, too, to revisit the coastal resort of San Benedetto del Tronto, where we had strolled almost alone in April. This time the beach was crowded with thousands of holidaymakers, but as we walked along the shore, we did not hear a single radio or raised voice. It was in sharp contrast to a crowded English beach.

Soaring costs

Once home in England, we had a chance to decipher the detailed schedule of works and breakdown of costs that Anna had, at last, handed us after transcribing the Fabios' Italian for us. She had also taken it from their lire into euros and we moved it on again into sterling.

To say that it came as a shock is to call the Assisi earthquake a minor tremor. The costs left us reeling. The original £32,000 renovation estimate that Anna had given us the previous September had more than doubled. She had told us then that the figure could obviously be only an approximation, that costs and prices could fluctuate and that any extras that we requested along the way would have to be added. Yet precious little on this list of costs at which we now stared in disbelief were items that we had construed as being extras. We were dumbfounded and our bemusement was not helped when we went in detail through the sixty-plus items on the schedule. The labour costs were as high as in England and the price of such items as doors, windows and shutters was far higher.

A hundred thoughts raced through our minds. Had we been tricked? Not by Anna, we were fairly certain, but had the builders perhaps seen us as a pair of gullible foreigners ripe for overcharging? Perhaps Anna had pressed a wrong button on her calculator at the very start? Could it be that Rosie and I, our vision and objectivity blurred by our excitement over the whole venture, had misinterpreted somewhere along the line? Despite our many shortcomings, we were certain that the last of these was not the case as our journalistic background had pretty well ensured the accuracy of our note-taking.

Written exchanges with Anna quickly ensued, the friendship that had existed between us suddenly tainted by our distress and anger. The builders were expected back on site in a couple of weeks, as soon as official go-ahead had been received from the local authority and the Fabios had completed a stopgap job they had taken on to tide them over. We asked Anna to tell them to await our instructions before returning to Casa Rosa. She was adamant that we had either misunderstood her or that we should at the very least have expected the costs to have soared. We were just as determined that the blame lay with her for not signalling this shock news. Never once did we see it coming. Dealing with the extra cost was enough of a blow, we explained, but the root cause of our anger was Anna's failure to warn us.

The more questions we asked, the more muddied the waters became, and the geographical distance between us, necessitating that communication was done by post or email, was not helping to make things clearer. But as the messages whizzed back and forth between Wiltshire and Le Marche, certain details started to emerge.

There is not a shadow of doubt in my mind that the majority of the blame lay with Anna. Her lack of professionalism in the way she ran her business was at first quite endearing. We comforted ourselves with the certain knowledge that she was a decent, honest person well versed in the Italian way and fluent in its language. But now we were being seriously financially threatened by what we believed was almost certainly her incompetence.

The nub of the problem seemed to lie in the interpretation of extras. Of all that had been discussed involving Anna, Vincenzo, the Fabios and us, the only items that Rosie and I had considered to be extras were the studio and swimming pool projects, both of which were intended to come later and neither of which was included in the estimate; some terracing and shade-creating pergolas, also not referred to in the price; and a small downstairs bathroom, which was included.

From Anna's viewpoint, though, the extras also included demolition of the pigsty and bread oven, construction of a new kitchen in their place, far more extensive repair and replacement work on the roof, ceilings and floors than had been anticipated, as well as some additional strengthening work and other detailed items demanded by a picky council official. Reconnecting essential services like electricity and water was also going to be pricey. With hindsight it was clear that the changeover from the lira to the euro had also played a part.

However the misunderstandings had occurred, the unpalatable fact remained that to turn our little hillside hovel into a habitable home was going to set us back nearer £70,000 than the £32,000 we had budgeted for, and even then there would be no pool, no studio, no terrace. Kitchen and bathroom fittings would also have to be paid for separately – another area of misunderstanding – and then we would have to furnish the place.

The village of Montottone.

It was no use flinging blame or wringing hands. Anger would not drive the problem away. A way forward had to be found and ours was to seek, with the help of Lorella and Oreste at Montottone, another estimate for the work on our house. Anna agreed that this was a sensible move. If the figure came in somewhere near the Fabios' costs, we would probably tell them to proceed with the work as we were content with the quality of their workmanship. If a new quote undercut them by a significant amount, then we would entrust new builders with our treasured little house, even if it meant further delays.

Why, we privately wondered, had we not insisted on additional estimates at the start? Had the house been in our own country, we certainly would have done. With hindsight, we should also have demanded to see an estimate and full breakdown of costs from the Fabios long ago, certainly well before they started any work. We had abandoned our normal caution, or common sense, as far as Casa Rosa was concerned, perhaps feeling we were buying the whole package from Anna. This was the way it worked in Le Marche and it had never occurred to us to challenge it. We trusted her judgement and experience, and we would follow the route down which she led us. Our private embarrassment at such profound confessions probably contributed to the subtle shift of our emotions from fury to frustration.

Before too long, despite worries over costs and the acrid aftertaste of our skirmish with Anna, we now felt curiously sanguine about everything. We had unshackled ourselves from our jobs, and our confidence, far from shrivelling as it might have done, was as high as it had ever been. Knowing that we were moving to a new house in Dorset, we had stopped clearing out belongings that we would rather keep. Casa Rosa would be furnished simply and modestly, with items bought locally. Time is one commodity in which we are suddenly rich.

The building site that would eventually become our Italian home.

The initial shock at the escalating costs had subsided. We had always built a huge helping of caution into our sums. The money will stretch and we shall press on with Casa Rosa regardless. If in a year or two we have to tweak our loosely woven plans for our lives, then so be it. Italy in June had been so absolutely wonderful that now we are doubly determined to live out our dream.

The lure of our Italian hillside seemed stronger than ever. Look around, we told ourselves. It is July in Wiltshire and again we looked out of our windows at torrential rain. Property values in Le Marche were rising even more quickly than all the experts were telling us. For the sum we paid to buy Casa Rosa, we could get nothing now. So if we had to economise a tad or go to work once in a while then that was what must happen. It would be fine. It would all work out.

The second estimate from local builders matched that of the Fabios closely enough to convince us that we should stick with them and we gave the go-ahead for work to resume. Atrocious late-summer weather caused further delays, but by the start of September 2002, the scaffolding was finally in place and the structural work got underway.

A lovely old farm cart, built in 1948 and beautifully hand-painted. The builders discovered it when they cleared the detritus from the ground floor.

Finished at last

Our next visit to Le Marche came in October 2002 when we again stayed at the *pensione*. Good progress had at last been made on the house. For the first time we were able to walk freely inside. Upstairs the floors had been replaced, the big bedroom created by the demolition of a wall, the opening for the stairs had been made and the dimensions of the smaller bedroom and upstairs bathroom had been identified. Downstairs the central wall had been strengthened and the archways created between the two rooms. A doorway had been opened on the western side to gain access to the area where the kitchen would eventually be constructed.

If we were cheered and encouraged by what we had seen that autumn, it was a different story on our next trip in the spring of 2003. The last snow of the winter had struck on the day prior to our visit but our arrival coincided with that of the summer and we enjoyed brilliant sunny days, becoming increasingly hot throughout our stay. Disappointingly little progress had been made on the house. Our south-facing meadow took its first step towards becoming what we hoped would be an orchard when we planted ten fruit trees: cherries, apricots, peach, pear and fig.

It was June 2003 before we spent our first night in Casa Rosa – a full year later than we had expected when we originally shook hands on the purchase twenty-one months earlier. If we thought at the time that we had been unlucky and felt a little hard done by, subsequent experience has taught us that this was far from true. Over budget and behind schedule seem to be par for the course in most of southern Europe; all that varies is the extent of the overruns.

With completion due at last, we set off in a high-top Transit van, laden with furniture and fittings, to drive the 1,200 miles from Dorset to Montottone. We had checked and double-checked with Anna that all would be finished by the time we got to the house and received categorical assurances. The Fabios, she said, were looking forward to our arrival and were happily anticipating our thrilled reactions.

On June 19, on the final morning of our long, tiring van journey, we phoned Anna from our overnight hotel in the far north of Italy to say we expected to arrive around one o'clock. She surprised us by saying that she was busy elsewhere and would not be able to meet us today. We were especially dismayed because the date had long been fixed. However, she would phone the Fabios to tell her our expected arrival time. At one o'clock, hot, tired, hungry but ridiculously excited, we trundled down the steep track to Casa Rosa but there was no sign of the Fabios' truck. Or, come to that, the Fabios. There was a labourer of eastern European origin, who seemed alarmed to see us but managed to explain, mostly with gestures, that the Fabios had gone to lunch. The Fabios, it seemed, go to lunch around 12.30 every day.

The interior of the house still resembled a building site; the sun was overhead and the heatwave was at its peak, so we parked our truck in the only area that provide a little shade and waited, our elation evaporating rapidly and turning, via impatience and frustration, into full-on fury. We had driven for four days, mostly in murderous heat; they all knew we were coming and when we were due to arrive, yet Anna suddenly had other business and the Fabios had gone to lunch.

Two hours later they arrived, wreathed in smiles. We had neither the language skills nor, by this time, the appetite to express the depth of our dismay. Suffice to say we waited another two hours while they and their slow-witted and slow-paced labourer cleared the worst of the detritus from inside the house.

Job done: the two Fabios prepare to leave.

Then they drove off home, leaving the two of us to carry our furniture and other belongings from the van into the hot, dusty house. We needed to draw on all our inner fortitude to prevent ourselves either screaming or weeping. A British builder would never have gone off like that and left us, we said, several times.

The Fabios were on site for the next five days, mostly working outside. We grew fond of them but were very happy when finally they said they were finished and we had Casa Rosa to ourselves. The heatwave, with temperatures topping 100F at times, lasted throughout our stay, and accompanied us and our hired van most of the way back to England.

The main bedroom at the newly restored Casa Rosa.

* * * * *

For the next ten years, Casa Rosa and Italy brought us an unpredictable blend of delight and despair, bemusement and enrichment; we had experiences, some truly wonderful, many quite surreal, that we would never have had if we had not embarked on our Italian adventure. There were many times when we seriously considered relocating permanently to Italy, and as many others, especially when we had skirmished with bureaucracy, when we wanted to zoom back to the comparative sanity of the UK.

We had never really formed a clear picture of how we would use Casa Rosa and whether we would try and obtain an income from it in the form of lettings. We were probably veering towards the idea of keeping it solely for our own use, knowing the option of letting it out to paying guests was something we may call on at a later date.

However, so hard were we hit financially by the huge and unexpected overspend on the renovation that we decided that the house owed us some sort of payback, at least for a while, so in the latter part of 2003 and much of 2004, we let out Casa Rosa, although only to friends. It worked quite well and generated a decent contribution to our costs. By the autumn of 2004, however, we decided that we wanted to use the house more ourselves and the complication of preparing for and dealing with guests was not worth the trouble.

During the years of our ownership, we stayed at the house sixty-seven times, for periods ranging from four or five days to almost a month. Yes, I did keep count, and I also kept a diary of our activities, experiences and emotions. All were memorable and most were positive but more than a few were not. Bureaucracy, weather, wildlife, the vagaries of an old house embedded in the countryside – they all contributed to the bad bits. But the friendships, the food, the landscapes and the craziness more than balanced the books.

Italy is different things to different people and every foreigner will tell a different story. I'll tell you some of ours.

Secondo

The war with nature

The trouble with nature is that it can turn ugly. One minute you're gawping in admiration and awe at its beauty, the next you're running for cover as it bares its teeth and comes after you. When nature declares war, it usually wins.

We know now, with the perfect clarity of hindsight, that we probably bought the wrong sort of house. Because we were not permanently in residence, we should have chosen somewhere that was not going to be left at nature's mercy for weeks on end, what some estate agents call a 'lock up and leave' property. It should have been an apartment with a terrace or two for outside space and it should have been in a town or village.

We had been seduced by the amazing views that Casa Rosa offered us. Wrapped in some of Le Marche's famously rich countryside, there was beauty out of every window, tranquillity came, usually, as standard, and the little house possessed a modesty and an honesty that we adored.

Casa Rosa, with the beautiful Le Marche countryside all around it and the snow-topped Sibillini Mountains in the distance.

When nature was benign, it was staggeringly beautiful. The fields and little woodland areas around us were a kaleidoscope of colour as the seasons passed: blood-red poppies in the grassland and banks, fields a blaze of sunflowers, shy purple orchids and cyclamen in our little copse, trees laden with peaches and apricots. An apple tree that we planted rewarded us with two oddly shaped apples, its entire harvest over several years, but we were proud of having grown them.

Half of our total apple crop. We were so proud.

We would often see hoopoes pecking around in search of food, huge golden eagles would cruise down the valley from the direction of the mountains, sometimes coming low enough to distinguish their feathers until, usually, being seen off by a posse of angry, defensive crows. One summer we spotted a golden oriole and even had the thrill of seeing on our land a flock of vividly coloured little birds that we identified as bee-eaters. On summer evenings, the air would sparkle with darting fireflies, tiny iridescent jewels, while we were serenaded throughout the nights by the soulful, liquid song of nightingales. One evening we spotted a porcupine, surely as dramatic-looking creature as Italy possesses, other than perhaps a few of its television presenters. During supper one night, we heard noises from outside the back and opened it to find a huge hedgehog parked there.

A night-time visitor waits by the back door.

Rosie wrote this in the summer of 2013:

Nature stars in the view from here

In this paradise where we find ourselves, halfway down the back of Italy's leg, there is much to amuse and entertain without so much as shifting our position on the terrace.

To shift is to expend effort. That is not a good thing and is, surely, not what total holiday relaxation is about. Admittedly, dawn till dusk indolence grows wearisome after the first day or two, and any longer than that could give one the idea that a holiday is not much more than pure boredom. So building in some regular activity, like a beach walk or a visit to somewhere interesting, helps us feel better about the whole indolence thing and keeps the old blood moving along in the way it's apparently meant to.

The principal activity, though, if that could possibly be the word I dare use, is in sitting and observing from the terrace, looking over the vineyard and the olives, across the little oak wood, beyond the honey-coloured medieval villages perched like scattered cake decorations on hilltops all the way to the distant mountains, some still striped with late-spring snow.

There is nothing to see, just landscape. Yet there is so much to see. The view changes by the second. It holds our gaze for such lengths of time that hours drift by and we find we've done nothing but drink in the beauties and wonders of the Italian countryside.

There are no people visible, just Nature at its most pure, getting on with the business of daily life. We see small pictures, perhaps a line of ants route-marching purposefully to a corner of the terrace or a green and tan gecko scuttling across the grass, and we see large dramas that fill our vision, such as a questing bird of prey being mobbed by crows or a piece of farm machinery making patterns as it cuts fields of grass. Later, more patterns will appear when the hay is gathered into huge bales to sit and bake in the sun.

It is probably the birds that give us the most pleasure. There can be nothing to match the golden river of song delivered night and day by the nightingales that surround the house. We don't see them, and since they are but drab, brown little things, this could be just as well, for I visualise them as nothing less than brilliant jewels shimmering somewhere just out of sight.

Something distinctly jewel-like revealed itself to us the other day: a bee-eater, no less, masquerading as an escapee from an exotic aviary.

Then there are the eagles. They make the flight from the mountains – not far as the noisy crow flies – to deliver the most extraordinary aerial displays, dipping, rising, weaving, sending small birds into a frenzy of warning screeches and making everything look small and vulnerable, ourselves included. Once, one rose from the valley on a thermal and landed close to the house. It looked, with its wings outstretched as it got its balance, for all the world like a large man in fancy dress, something one doesn't see that often in remote Italian gardens.

Starlings are fairly ubiquitous birds, and suddenly, on Monday, there were about a million of the things arguing and squabbling among themselves like coarse teenagers as they stretched their wings and took tentative solo flights from the roof.

I knew, without checking the date, that it would be 10th June, because that's when birds fly the nest, or so my mother always told me. How funny to find that even in the Euro zone they should do the same.

A sunny day at Casa Rosa.

But if nature delivered us so many wonderful gifts, it also brought torments. Prominent among them were very small, very invasive flies or midges, known by the locals as *pappataci*. We never encountered mosquitoes during all our time at Casa Rosa, there being no water close by, but the even smaller *pappataci* were almost as bad and an even more determined and furtive enemy. In our early years at the house, we did not have a problem but, as the years went on, they became an ever greater nuisance. Sitting outside was a constant risk in all but the coldest weather; you'd feel a slight itch, move to scratch it and see a small, red spot, which would get increasingly irritating as the hours passed. The flies were so small that, often, they were invisible to us and so sneaky that, unlike mosquitoes, they did not alert us to their presence with the high-pitched buzz. They would bite you in exposed places such as your face and hands, but they would also get you through your socks. Some were small enough to go straight through ordinary fly screens and into the house. Moving the air with high-speed fans made little difference; neither did citronella candles, fly swats, sprays, twelve-bore shotguns or coating your body in fly repellent. We wondered why they had got so much worse over the years of our ownership. Climate change? Or maybe something to do with the chemicals that the *contadini* farmers were spraying? The things were invincible and, in truth, became one of our biggest nuisances during the latter part of our time at Casa Rosa.

If the *pappataci* were the most insistently troublesome of nature's army of occupation, they certainly were not alone. Small black scorpions often appeared around the house and had to be carefully removed; we never received a sting from one but their presence could be quite unsettling. Outside we were often troubled by wasps, apparently more insistent than back home in England. Once or twice we were visited by black snakes, supposedly not poisonous but, at four feet long, large enough to send us scuttling for cover. One year the grassed area immediately behind the house fell victim to moles. First one hill appeared, then another and then it tuned into a plague. Each morning we would look out and more hills had been created. After a week or two, there was more hill than grass until eventually it stopped as suddenly as it had begun. Was it a whole tribe of moles or just one rogue? Who knew? That's the thing about moles – you can never be sure.

A rather larger pest that appeared from time to time and caused massive havoc was wild boar. We would spot them from time to time wandering around in our little vineyard area, looking a bit like mini rhinoceros and just as ungainly. They never came close when we were around but on several occasions we saw evidence of their visits in the form of grubbed-up areas of ground and destroyed shrubs and plants. It made me feel less uncomfortable when I saw wild boar on a restaurant menu.

A wild boar looking for food in the vineyard.

Omnipresent lizards were not a nuisance, more a form of entertainment, scuttling around all around the garden area, occasionally falling with a plop from the guttering on the terrace roof and darting away, startled and confused. Sometimes we would find one or two inside the house, looking bewildered and limp, having exhausted themselves trying to find a way out. Once, on opening the front of the woodburning stove to light it one spring, a tired, cold and hungry lizard stared back at us. It had obviously fallen down the chimney. Goodness knows how long it had been there because it put up no struggle at all when I picked it up to eject it, but after five minutes outside in the sunshine, it was full of verve again and showing no ill-effects.

A bewildered lizard awaits rescue from the woodburner.

Nature's airborne assault troops took the form of the world's
most noisy starlings, which somehow drilled their way under
the ridge tiles and lived in the roof. They would wake well
before dawn every day and hold rave events immediately
above our bedroom. The scratching of their clawed feet and
boisterous scuffling provided an unattractive wake-up call
each morning. Men with ladders and wire charged us a
fortune for supposedly blocking up all the likely entry points
each winter but somehow the starlings outsmarted us every
year.

But the starlings, the wild boar, the spiteful little *pappataci*
flies, the moles, even the snakes – they were mere skirmishes
compared with the worst of the lot: hornets. Three times they
declared war on us during our time at Casa Rosa.

From small beginnings: a hornet starts building its nest on the outside of the house. Fortunately we spotted this one and dealt with it swiftly.

Their first arrival came in September of 2004. My sister and her family were to come out and stay with us for a few days to celebrate her birthday. Half a dozen of our relatives were also flying out to join the fun, staying at Lorella's *pensione* and spending their days with us at Casa Rosa.

A few days before their scheduled arrival, we noticed the presence of the hornets. They were huge, like great pumped-up bees but much larger, louder and more threatening. They were following a clear flight-path into and out of one of the innumerable gaps in the brickwork at the back of the house. Fortunately their chosen site was high up so their flight took them well above our heads but the numbers were growing steadily each day. The arrival and departure route was becoming less like a gently buzzing passage and more like a frantic rush-hour crowd. Venturing outside in to the back garden was increasingly unnerving.

Bees in Italy are a protected species; hornets, thankfully, are not. But they are formidable enemies and horror stories abound. Don't confront them and they will not attack, we were assured by knowledgeable locals. There were tales of brave souls who, armed presumably with massive swats and goodness knows what else, have gone into battle with hornets and ended up hospitalised. Even deaths are not unknown. A swarm of hornets is not an easy foe.

Our relatives' arrival occurred a few days before the hornet drama reached full power but they were enough of a scary presence to ensure that a fair area of our garden was out of bounds. The sight of thousands of hornets zooming backwards and forwards a few feet above our heads, into and out of their home in our bricks, was a constant, worrying distraction. Our garden was hardly an area for relaxation. Once our guests had returned to England, we could focus on what was to be done about the hornets. We were fortunate in that our friendship with Lorella had led to us also becoming well acquainted with her wonderful parents, a wise and warm couple with whom we felt we had established a firm bond despite their inability to speak English. At that time our Italian was rudimentary at best.

Mario was a countryman through and through. He understood the workings of Italian wildlife better than anyone we knew and had experienced so much at first-hand during his seventy-plus years. He was also as fit and athletic as a man half his age and was never happier than either tackling some daunting physical task or helping some hapless neighbour. With us he often had the chance to combine both.

The hornets had to be halted, he said, or they would continue to return to the same nest. The cavity in the brickwork where they had built their nest and the holes that they used as their entry and exit points had to be sealed. He had Styrofoam, an applicator, a big ladder, a protective suit and mask and he would do it, he said.

The next morning, we were woken just after six by the sound of a vehicle and quickly realised it was Mario heading home, having come to the house and carried out his heroic task while we slept. Outside we saw that the holes in the wall had been plugged with pink foam (why had we expected white? This was Italy, after all). There were also chunks of solidified foam on the ground and a fair number of confused hornets circling the rear of the house, clearly wondering what had happened to their front door and their families while they were out.

So problem solved then? Well, not quite. Whether Mario's onslaught had not filled all the cavity or whether there had been far more entrance tunnels than expected, it is hard to say, but it took Mario two more pre-dawn raids and a fair bit more pink foam before the hornet invasion was properly put to flight.

Despite the fact that the air all around Casa Rosa seemed permanently abuzz with flying things, it was to be another seven years before our next close encounter with hornets. And, believe me, it really was close.

It was late October 2011 and as we drove onto our land at the start of what would be a 17-day stay, we immediately noticed the presence of the most horrible-looking thick brown stains down the front wall of the house. They looked like the darkest treacle and seemed to be emanating from one of the large east-facing windows of our bedroom. What on earth had happened?

The nightmare sight of a hornets' nest built between the glass and the shutters of one of our bedroom windows.

A few minutes later, we opened the door into our bedroom and saw nothing amiss – until we opened the shutters on the other windows to allow the light to flood in. The sight that met our eyes was scarcely imaginable. In the window from which the vile gunge appeared to have come, the cavity between the glass and the shutters had been filled, from top to bottom, with a hornets' nest from hell. Fortunately the windows were tightly sealed so nothing had come into our bedroom. But the nest was absolutely vast: more than three feet high and two wide, an extraordinarily intricate artwork made of brown, cardboard-like material and swarming with sluggish hornets, whose dark retreat had suddenly been illuminated by our arrival.

The brown slime on the outside walls was the insects' bodily fluids, and while none of the stuff – nor the hornets – had entered our room, an acrid, unpleasant smell was evident close to the window. The only way to open the shutters and smash this vast nest would have been to open the windows and invite the creatures to come in and murder us in our own bedroom; we felt it was probably not a prudent course of action.

So we left it alone. We were assured that the hornets would die off over winter and, as there did not seem to be another option, we decided we would have to rely on that being so. We slept in the room for the next 17 nights, with the ghastly nest only a couple of feet away from our bed. We ignored the pungent aroma from their giant nest and returned to England for the winter, hoping that the problem would solve itself in our absence.

Happily it did. When we next drove onto the site in early April 2012, not only had the hornets vanished – there were no live ones around but countless corpses on the ground far below – but so, too, had the revolting river of hornet poo that had so disfigured the house last year. We suspected that the vast community of ants that lived nearby and regularly marched up and down that wall was responsible for the clean-up.

All we had to do was, gingerly, to open the windows inside the bedroom, break through the crumbling nest and open the shutters. We flung the intricately worked chunks of nest down to the ground below and embarked on the time-consuming task of clearing and cleansing the window, shutters and cavity. The relief of having our window back in use and clear of the hornet infestation was immense. Our poor little house had been reclaimed again.

The respite, however, turned out to be quite short-lived. The first sign of invasion number three came towards the end of our August 2013 visit. Casa Rosa has a little outside cupboard affair, a shed-size space built beneath the external staircase and with a door next to and at right-angles to the front door into the house. It is a place where we kept 'stuff': log basket, kindling, half-empty paint cans, a few rarely used garden tools that wouldn't fit into the main shed, that sort of thing. A few days before heading back to England, we spotted a small number of hornets building a nest on the cupboard ceiling. It looked a bit like half a coconut shell and was about that size. After our previous experience, it rang alarm bells with us but how best to tackle the problem? There were enough hornets involved in the construction to rule out the possibility of a full frontal assault but not enough yet to be truly daunting.

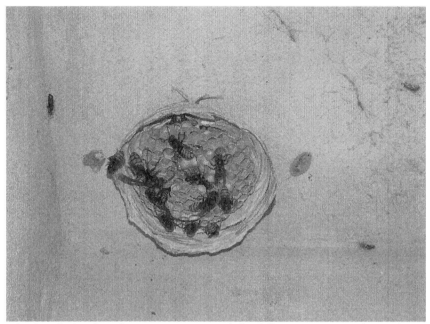

The battle begins: hornets start work building a nest on the ceiling of our shed.

Phase one, we decided, would be to close the cupboard door (it was usually left open during our spells in residence). The creatures inside would probably die off and their mates would be unable to get in to help with the construction work. Phase one failed in minutes. The wonky old door was a poor fit and the hornets simply carried on untroubled, gaining access over and under the doorway.

Phase two, therefore, would have to be carried out under cover of darkness when the beasts would be asleep. It involved creeping outside with a small torch – not using the outside light as that would have woken them – and using heavy-duty parcel tape to seal around the cupboard door. By next morning these striped monsters had eaten, sliced or blowtorched a hole in the tape and the winged traffic in and out of the cupboard was progressing at its usual speed.

A second application of tape the following night was treated with similar disdain and, by now, we were running out of ideas and time. We were also wondering what sort of size the nest had reached by this stage. Our plane was beckoning so we had no option but to accept that they may have won the early skirmishes but we would be back in three weeks and they had better watch out.

The massive, swirling dark shape near the front door of Casa Rosa as we arrived for our next stay three weeks later told us that the Hornet War Three had been declared. It was a blood-tingling sight: thousands, maybe tens of thousands of the animals swarming around the door of the cupboard that we had tried and failed to make hornet-proof three weeks earlier. The bombardment from the skies made that side of the house completely out of bounds for anyone without a suit of armour so we entered by the back door.

Peering nervously through the windows, we were dumbstruck at the sheer scale of the problem. The air was dark with hornets whizzing in and out of the cupboard from all directions. They obviously had evil in their hearts and were hellbent on avenging the deaths of their ancestors that Mario had walled up nine years earlier. So we kept the windows shut tight, used the back door for our escape route and agreed that we needed reinforcements if we were to see off this persistent foe and be able to survive the next fortnight without a trip to the hospital emergency room.

Cristina, our nearest neighbour, a woman with many years' experience of life immersed in Le Marche's beautiful, challenging countryside, would be able to help. She would summon the cavalry for us and, importantly, would know their phone number. Dealing with hornet infestations, apparently, was the responsibility of the fire brigade. Explaining our predicament on the phone was going to be a big ask for us so Cristina called them for us. To our utter astonishment, not only did they understand the problem and say they would be with us within an hour to deal with the problem, but they really were.

If their response and rapid deployment overjoyed us, in a way that so many events in Italy did when you least expected them to, then the next few hours were so extraordinary, so totally surreal, that they will live long in our memories.

Less than an hour after Cristina's phone call, a full-sized scarlet fire engine bounced and wobbled its way down our narrow, rutted track and on to our land. Two firefighters climbed out of the truck and greeted us warmly, even enthusiastically, and assured us, with untypical Italian calmness, that everything would be fine. They would deal with the *calabroni*. We were ordered to go back into the house, shut all doors and windows (don't worry about that, we thought); we did as we were told and watched the action. The older, heftier of the men settled himself comfortably in the driver's seat of his truck and read his newspaper. The younger, fitter-looking one was obviously going to be the warrior-in-chief. First he climbed into a head-to-toe suit of protective clothing, including, of course, a face visor. He looked like a visitor from space. Then, clutching a black bin bag that we had provided, and armed with a hornet-busting chemical spray, he walked calmly through the swarm, opened the cupboard and simply walked in.

For us, watching the drama unfold from the safety of our house, it was like seeing a full-size action movie literally on our own doorstep. There was a giant rumpus going on in our little cupboard as man and hornet battled for supremacy. Now and then we would see his arm swiping and swinging as the battle raged. It was like a cartoon show. At one point he emerged to indicate to us that the nest had been more than a metre across. Soon the bin bag was flung to the floor near our front door; it contained the smashed sections of nest and a vast number of dead hornets.

Finally our firefighter emerged, triumphant. Do you have a fly swat, he asked? All we had was a wimpy little pink plastic one, barely strong enough to bruise a mosquito, but he seemed happy enough with it. Back into battle he went, wielding the fly swat like a tennis pro wields a racquet. To say it was an incongruous sight would be to understate it. He swatted dozens of dazed and disorientated hornets that were still swirling around but soon the air was almost clear.

Finally he left the bin bag for us to dispose of, and assured us that the operation had been totally successful. He asked us to sign a few documents, said there would be no charge for the visit and politely declined either a coffee or a tip. Then he returned to the truck, woke his sidekick and they drove away into the sunset. It had been less than two hours since Cristina made that phone call and the nightmare on Via del Colle was over.

Hero: firefighter, clad head to toe in a protective suit, evicts the hornets.

Customer care?

The timetable attached to the ticket office wall at Porto San Giorgio railway station said the next train to Ancona was due to leave at 10.40am. We had studied it carefully and the message was unambiguous. Anyway, we had caught the 10.40 before and knew we were right.

The woman behind the screen, however, told a different story. The next train for Ancona, she insisted, was due to leave at 11.19. But there was supposed to be a 10.40; the timetable said as much, didn't it? She agreed that that was indeed the case but said simply, for the third or fourth time, that there is not a 10.40 train today for no reason whatsoever.

Understanding that, in Italy, there is absolutely no point in asking 'why?' was something we gathered very early in our relationship with the country, yet so often we were so taken aback by something that we still questioned it. Usually, however, if there is an explanation, it is one that leaves you more bewildered than you started so it is best to let it lie.

On this particular encounter at the railway station, we were in our fairly short-lived train-to-the-airport phase of returning to the UK. Most journeys involved driving to the airport at Ancona and either returning a hire car or putting our own car in long-term parking or leaving it with friends until our next visit. This latest idea involved leaving our car at Casa Rosa, getting a friend to give us a lift to the nearest railway station, Porto San Giorgio, and taking the train to Ancona. Last month it had worked smoothly; this time the train had been cancelled, with no advance warning and no subsequent explanation.

In the end it mattered little as we caught the 11.19, which was a faster train, and made it in good time for our flight. But the whole episode, which caused a disproportionately high level of stress and frustration, perfectly summed up much of day-to-day life in Italy and the Italians' singular interpretation of customer care.

Like so many aspects of Italian life, the concept of customer care is a complex and unpredictable thing. In all our years there, we rarely left a shop or office without reflecting on our treatment, which may have been appalling beyond belief or brilliant beyond compare.

Specialist shops tended to be particularly trying places. We visited quite a few, especially in our early days when we were still buying odds and ends to furnish the house or acquire replacements for fittings that had failed. We came to realise that an expedition to buy even the simplest item from an ironmonger, a furniture store, or a bathroom or kitchen showroom meant writing off a whole day. One errand, one day – that was usually the way of things.

First it was important to fathom the chosen shop's bizarre and illogical opening hours. If it was a saint's day, some other public holiday or, heaven forbid, August, then forget it. If the transaction involved seeking advice and may take a while, then it was vital to arrive early as lunch took priority over everything. Twelve o'clock meant lunch, even if that involved ushering customers out of the door. No matter that the customer was holding a fat bundle of cash and threatening to go to a competitor down the road - lunchtime meant the shop was closing. *Chiuso!* The very concept of competitiveness does not appear to have reached provincial Italy.

If we were fortunate enough to find our chosen shop open and interested in doing business, there was every chance that we would have become invisible. Certainly the sales people could not possibly see us because, if they had, surely they would have looked up and acknowledged our presence, even if actually greeting us and offering to help was asking too much of them.

If we were lucky, Anna-Maria or Tiziana would eventually make a grunting noise to indicate that they were prepared to listen to our request; sometimes, although seldom, they would even look up from their computer screens briefly. Usually, partway through our efforts to explain our requirements, Tiziana's cellphone would ring and, of course, she would answer it. Several more minutes would pass while pleasantries were exchanged with the caller and arrangements for tonight's date were finalised.

She would then look back at us, apparently surprised that we were still there, and invite us to explain everything again. Without giving the faintest clue as to whether or not she could supply our needs, she would then turn back to her beloved computer and trawl through page after page of data, before looking back and, inevitably, saying no. No, she didn't have the item; if she had it, it would take another hour to discover the price; no, she didn't know when or even if she would be getting some in; nor could she suggest where else we might try to get it; and actually, it was now lunchtime, she wanted to close and would we mind awfully buggering off as we were seriously disturbing her work.

If anyone thinks this description is a gross exaggeration, then they obviously haven't tried using an ironmonger, a furniture store, a bathroom or kitchen supplier in rural Italy. And still they complain that business is slow and that there is no money around. It will be the government's fault.

There are countless examples of shops and businesses who appear to regard paying customers as an irritating intrusion into their working day, the main point of which is to stare at computer screens, shuffle forests of paper around, strut ostentatiously and self-consciously around offices or showrooms and basically fill in the gaps between meals.

Two of the planet's most appalling companies, however, deserve particular mentions. The first of these is Banca Marche. Some expat friends of ours in the region have found them to be perfectly efficient and courteous, but they did not use the same branch that we did. It was in the small town of Grottazzolina a few miles away.

If you were fortunate enough to arrive during one of the very short and illogical windows that purported to be opening hours, the next ordeal was negotiating your way through a glass-walled kiosk just about large enough for one person (it would be of little use in obesity dominated Britain). Bags had to be deposited and buttons pressed before you were finally disgorged into the bank. Usually we failed at this stage and had to be rescued by some unsmiling and unsympathetic staff member whose salary was paid thanks to the bank charges we had to cough up.

Once inside the main part of the bank, we had to join a queue – or what passes for a queue in Italy; more a loose milling about of people on their mobile phones. There may be ten people waiting to be served, four or five counter positions and one person actually in place. Four or five others would be wandering around behind the counter, very slowly, carrying sheaves of paper or just chatting loudly. Most of the staff wore jeans; none of them looked at their customers and certainly none of them ever smiled.

Once you got to the front of the queue, there was usually a wait until the cashier looked up from his or her screen. There was always – always – a sneer. Out of bloody-mindedness born of experience, we did not speak until the cashier did; that, at least, made them acknowledge our presence. After we explained our request, they would, typically, get up from their seat and walk away. Were they dealing with our request? Were they fetching a supervisor because they couldn't understand what these annoying Brits wanted? Had they gone to the lavatory? Or to lunch? Or simply become bored and needed to go and phone their mother to find out what was on the menu for *pranzo*? Who could tell?

Mostly they could not help us, nor could they advise us who would and actually, it was now lunchtime, they wanted to close and would we mind awfully buggering off. Yes, we really grew to love Banca Marche.

The second of the two worst companies on the face of the earth was TIM, providers of phone, mobile and internet services if you were very, very lucky. Over the years, we grew to despise TIM with a degree of hatred of which we had not thought ourselves capable.

Our first contact with them was to buy an Italian sim card that we could put into our mobile phone during each visit to Italy and top up as and when necessary. We were accompanied on that errand by our Italian friend Oreste and it went smoothly. We did not know it at the time, of course, but that visit turned out to be the only one of our many millions of contacts with TIM, right through to the present day, that went without a hitch.

Next was a visit to another TIM shop to buy a dongle to use with our laptop so that we could work, send and receive emails and surf the net while in Italy. It was supposed to be a high-speed broadband dongle but it never worked at all at Casa Rosa and only at the speed of a geriatric snail if we took it to a hilltop in search of a signal. It was better than nothing but only just and it was expensive.

For the next few years, because of the irregularity of our visits, we found it necessary to buy credit, lasting a month, each time we arrived in Italy. TIM had obviously been tipped off about our arrival dates so every one of their stores would be closed. We had to return the next morning when there would be queues all around the shop and sometimes out into the street. When we reached the counter, they would close for lunch. When they reopened four hours later, they pretended not to understand what we wanted, but when they did finally capitulate and agree to sell us some more credit, the price had shot up. This was the story at all the branches we ever used and it happened to us about sixty times.

We no longer have to use dongles and laptops because technology, thank goodness, has moved on somewhat. Dealing with TIM over our cellphones, however, has been almost as frustrating and has gone on for many years. TIM are impossible to deal with by phone or face to face, their website never does what I plead with it to do, yet still we stick with them because switching to another company, such as the improbably named WIND, would probably take more years than I have left to live and anyway the others are supposedly just as bad. Do you wonder we hate TIM?

So many businesses we encountered during our years in Le Marche gave the clear impression that customers were little more than a necessary nuisance, an intrusion into their peaceful lives. It was certainly true of big companies, like banks and phone providers, but often it was a similar story with small family firms. Doubtless there was sometimes a certain nervousness in dealing with foreigners, even though we had a fair mastery of the language. In Le Marche, however, *stranieri* were often still viewed with apprehension or even suspicion.

Sometimes, though, the opposite was true. Some shop staff positively revelled in dealing with foreign customers and nothing was too much trouble. If they knew a few English phrases, as some of the younger ones did, then so much the better and they were keen to try it out. When service was good in Italy, it was truly brilliant and often gave us experiences that cheered us for days.

We had bought a rather smart floor-standing lamp from a specialist lighting shop during our initial furnishing spree at Casa Rosa. Several years later, the bulb blew. It was an unusual, expensive type so we returned to the same shop in the hope of obtaining a replacement. We were braced for a costly purchase but the friendly shopkeeper insisted that she remembered us from all those years earlier, handed us a new bulb and absolutely refused to take payment for it.

The man who ran a small but well-stocked ironmongery did not have the hose reel or garden tap that we had gone in to buy but drove out to us a couple of days later to deliver the items and, because we were regular customers, refused to take payment for the tap. He even fitted it for us.

Customer service that goes above and beyond was also provided by the company we employed to provide an annual service for our gas boiler. They would phone on the same day each year to notify us that the service was due and make arrangements to visit, and their technician would arrive, rain or shine, on the dot and carry out the service. It was always done in complete silence because he spoke no English and looked afraid when we attempted to make polite conversation in Italian. The work done, he would spend the next half-hour silently filling out paperwork by hand and gave us an unreadable receipt for the payment.

The service we always received from Fiamma, the butane gas suppliers, was every bit as impressive. We would phone them, often when we were almost down to the last fumes and there was snow on the ground, and they would send their huge truck down our bumpy track and top up our tank. Again, filling out the paperwork took longer than delivering the gas but the drivers were always punctual, reliable and friendly. Yes, for every TIM or Banca Marche, there was a Fiamma or an independent trader with a smile.

The one sector on which we could rely for brilliant service and outstanding quality virtually every single time was the food sector; in all our years of visiting Italy, it is hard to remember more than one or two occasions when we have been less than happy with a restaurant or café. The Italians have an enviable reputation for their food and take the most enormous pride in it. If it does dominate their lives and rule their rigid daily routines, then it's really not surprising.

Throttled by red tape

Ask a Brit who's never lived in Italy and the chances are he'll have no trouble listing the characteristics that make life in *Il Bel Paese* so wonderfully appealing. The fun-loving, smiling Italian people, for a start; their relaxed, happy-go-lucky approach to life; long lunches with amazing food and *vino*; a glorious, reliable, sunny climate; and a stress-free lifestyle where most things can wait until *domani*.

Many of us who have lived in Italy or owned a property there, however, will tell a different story. The contradictions between perception and reality could hardly be greater.

The Italians have allowed their bureaucrats to tie them up in more red tape than probably any other westernised country. Every single exercise seems to have been specially adapted and organised to make life almost impossibly tricky for ordinary people, especially disbelieving foreigners, while simultaneously creating tiers of unnecessary, unfulfilling and underpaid jobs.

It is a seemingly endless maze that most Italians don't understand and yet do not challenge, and a whole sub-culture has grown up comprising people who earn a good living by untangling the tape and enabling the nation to function. If these people also happen to be issued with a uniform, then frankly you'd be better off just forgetting the whole thing.

Italians are also imprisoned by an iron sense of routine. They go to the same shops on the same days, eat at the same time, the same food, and most of them, especially the older ones, would never countenance the idea of trying something different. A meal without pasta is not a meal for the average Italian. In our part of Italy, we were delighted to note that the only branch of McDonald's we knew was usually near-empty. They should have sold pasta-burgers!

In our early days at Casa Rosa, we invited some Italian friends for Sunday lunch and decided to offer a traditional English roast. They kept looking around to see if the pasta was on its way and were horrified when they tumbled that it wasn't. They hardly touched their food, played with their mobile phones throughout and raced off home as soon as they could, presumably to devour some spaghetti.

Relaxed and happy-go-lucky they certainly were not. The Italians whom we knew best were in a constant state of anxiety about their health. Hypochondria is prevalent in Italy, and they always seem to have a hand-me-down tale of an obscure remedy for some even more obscure condition.

Italy's obsession with red tape can be seen whenever you come into contact with officialdom. It may be buying a car, opening a bank account, buying or renting a house, trying to obtain a landline phone or a television, registering for a water or drainage supply, or arrange for electricity to be connected or disconnected. Nothing can be done in one smooth, slick operation. Often it is due to illogical opening hours, or because Antonio doesn't work Thursdays, or because the computer system is kaput, or because it's nearly lunchtime/weekend/a saint's day so it's not really worth embarking on this today and can you come back at 4.12pm on Friday fortnight. And every operation will involve a ton of paper, scores of signatures and your date and place of birth and mother's maiden name.

Nowhere was the collision with bureaucracy more annoying or frustrating, however, than on our numerous visits to the *comune*, the local council, housed in a large and impressive building in the centre of our small village. There were great porticos outside and the Italian flag hung limply over the imposing façade. An old bicycle and a small council van usually stood sentry.

Inside all was quiet. In the large entrance hall area, it had the air of a doctor's waiting room, the silence broken only by the occasional clacking of official heels on the tiled floors. There was usually a gathering of villagers looking either dead-eyed and resigned if they were Italians, or agitated to the point of explosive fury if they were foreigners. The handful of council staff could occasionally be heard behind closed doors speaking loudly into their phones, and, once in a while, one would emerge, determinedly avoid the pleading eyes of the gathered multitude, and dive off through another door.

Rosie and I spent many an hour in that building. Italians don't queue but they do take waiting to new heights. They'll wait in shops or at market stalls while the person being served continues a long, rambling discussion about the family, the neighbours, the television, the football and occasionally even about the items they are buying. Nothing persuades them to speed up their conversation or perhaps actually bring it to an end until they have completely run out of things to say. The posse of people a few centimetres behind them waiting to be served might as well not be there for all the notice they take. The great majority of our visits to the *comune* offices were about our ICI, later changed to IMU, roughly the Italian equivalent of council tax. The arrangements are different for each *comune* but ours in Montottone did not send out notices requesting payment, nor was it possible to pay other than by cash at the little post office just down the street. Direct debit? Bank transfer? No chance! What was possible was to go several years without paying a *centissimo* until the debt had built into something frightening; the onus was on the householders to pay their dues.

In the spring of 2006, almost five years after buying Casa Rosa and three years after completion of the restoration, we finally managed to register it for ICI. It had taken us countless visits to the offices of the *comune,* and the sense of triumph against enormous odds once we achieved our objective was indescribable. Naturally it was the usual Italian pantomime.

We had encountered the usual prevarication, excuses and incomprehension from the *comune* front-line staff so this time we asked to see the *sindaco* (the mayor). We were already on nodding and smiling acquaintance with Giuliano because we would often see him in *La Brocca* restaurant. He was a large, untidy, friendly man who had done a great deal of good things for Montottone and was highly regarded by everyone we knew.

Soon the *sindaco* descended from his first-floor office, greeted us warmly and invited us to follow him upstairs to his mayoral chamber. We were surprised by its size and grandeur for, although the building was large and impressive, the area it served certainly was not. In truth the *comune* was probably on a par with a large parish council in England. Giuliano's office was adorned with flags, ornaments and heavyweight furnishings, although it was difficult to make them out clearly because the whole chamber was thick with cigarette smoke. The *sindaco* was a serious, full-time smoker, rarely seen without a cigarette, and the overflowing ashtrays on his vast desk testified to the fact. In between the ashtrays were his phones.

We all coughed quite a lot. Giuliano spoke no English at all and our Italian was still quite rudimentary so progress was slow, confused and confusing. Our efforts to explain our mission were not helped either by the frequent explosions of mayoral coughing and the long pauses while a new cigarette was located and lit. Every now and then a minion would walk into the office, either to relay some message to the *sindaco* or to deliver a heap of papers on to his desk or, simply, to come and stare at the smoke-logged English couple.

Before and after this session in the mayor's office, we had witnessed numerous surreal happenings during our years in Italy, but this battle to be allowed to register our house for ICI and pay our bills was right up there with the most bizarre encounters.

After what seemed like hours, and actually was, Giuliano came up with an idea to break the deadlock; he would phone Cristina, our next-door neighbour, whose ceramics workshop was a few minutes' walk away, and ask her to come and interpret. She arrived a short while later, emerging through the smoke, and immediately lit a cigarette. The mayor, of course, followed suit. By this time we could hardly see across the room and, even though it was a fine spring day, the huge windows stayed firmly shut.

Cristina proved to be the key that unlocked the whole business. She explained to Giuliano that we had been trying for years to pay our dues on the house. He was full of sympathy and apologies. It would be dealt with immediately and there would be no question of our having to pay any arrears because it had not been our fault. The Montottone *comune* had let us down and he was very sorry indeed. Then he lit another cigarette and settled back in his enormous chair for a good cough. We staggered out of the mayoral chamber, drove home and fumigated our clothes.

If that encounter had finally enabled us to convince the *comune* that Casa Rosa existed and we were the owners, it was merely the start of our difficulties in paying the charges for the remaining seven years of our time as Le Marche property owners. It was payable in half-yearly instalments and it was necessary each time to visit the *comune* offices to obtain the necessary paperwork, then go to the post office to pay it. Sounds simple enough, doesn't it?

My notes, stained now with my sweat and tears, tell a sad story of failure. Daniela at the *comune* could never quite locate the right pieces of paper; when she did, she couldn't quite locate the correct amount for us to pay. We would have to come back at the same time next week because she only worked Thursdays. Next week came but Daniela was off work because of 'problems at home'. We thought she probably had not been able to locate the correct paperwork to get out of her front door. The following week we encountered the same story. Poor Daniela's domestic troubles continued. But then, of course, we had to return to England so it was another month before our next trip to the *comune*. And so it went on until we managed to obtain the right paperwork, with the correct amount at the seventh attempt. It was, however, five months into the six-month period so we would very soon need to start all over again.

In the event, it was to be the following spring before we returned to Italy and headed for the *comune* office again. We went on a Thursday but Daniela was off long-term. She was pregnant, we were told. So much for the 'problems at home'. We would have to deal instead with the lugubrious Marziano, an older man standing in for Daniela. He worked Mondays so we had to go back next week.

He could deal with everything for us but ICI had now changed to IMU which meant more work for him, more paperwork for everyone and frankly he didn't really know why he bothered. Nobody liked the change and hardly anyone paid anyway. Marziano did not seem happy in his work. We got the paperwork to pay the overdue portion but would have to come back in June for the new paperwork for the next payment. And we would have to come back again in December when the bill will have doubled for reasons we failed completely to understand but presumably the massive increase had been brought in mainly to make Marziano's unhappy, unfulfilled life even more miserable.

The following year, mercifully our last as home owners, we twice visited the *comune* offices to be told to come back in a few days. When we did so, the place was packed with people, including two fellow Brits whom we knew mainly from the local restaurant. They had been waiting over an hour, they told us, and were hovering somewhere between immense frustration and blind fury. When finally we got in to see Marziano, we were told the change to IMU had caused unprecedented chaos for the hardworking staff and we should return next week with the original receipt from last year's payment. God knows why.

Eventually we succeeded in paying what we owed but we were told there was no point even asking for the paperwork for the second half of 2013 because it was absolutely unthinkable that this could be produced. We would have to sort it all out when we returned in the spring of 2014. As things turned out, of course, we sold the house in late 2013 so never returned to Casa Rosa or the *comune* office in Montottone. I wonder if the paperwork has been prepared yet. If endeavouring to pay the tax on the house was the reason for the great majority of our visits to the *comune* offices, it certainly was not the only one. The condition of the 'white road' that led down to our house was one of the thorniest and most persistent problems that we wrestled with from the day we bought the house until the day we left.

The track was steep, uneven and rutted, and desperately susceptible to the weather conditions. At the top of the track was just one abandoned house; down at the foot of the hill were three properties: one was a rarely used second home belonging to an Italian; then there was Cristina's house, the only permanently occupied house; and finally Casa Rosa. There the road ended and beyond us was a vineyard and fields.

Most of the traffic was the *contadini* farmers, who would be on their tractors or in small trucks carrying mini diggers. Cristina drove up and down a couple of time most days and so did we when we were in residence. The road surface in winter was wickedly slippery, either with ice or, more often, deep wet mud churned by the farmers' vehicles. The sides of the narrow track fell away and sometimes collapsed completely, making the driving especially hazardous. In winter, Cristina often found herself cut off by snow for days at a time. In summer, with the track as hard as granite, the scars and holes in the surface could wreck your suspension at anything quicker than walking pace. Many was the time that we had woken to find there had been a night of heavy rain and we doubted whether we would be able to get up the track. Usually we did but it was a deeply anxious operation and a white-knuckle ride.

We had discussed the situation with a succession of mayors and agreement had been reached that, if the residents clubbed together to pay for the materials, the *comune* would send their entire team of one man to carry out the labour. It brings tears to my eyes to recall the convoluted and confusing discussions that we had on so many occasions, often with Cristina to add her weight to our pleadings. Once in a while the *comune* actually carried out some work but it was never the complete job and, because it was the mother of all botches, it never lasted for long. In truth the state of the track cast a shadow of varying depths over our lives throughout all of our years at Casa Rosa but the bureaucrats at the *comune* never came close to fulfilling their promises. It was a battle we were never destined to win.

A house in the country

The day we first clapped eyes on the decrepit little house that would eventually become Casa Rosa, we were captivated by its views. Le Marche, we knew, was all about views and dazzling, heart-lifting landscapes and this location had it all. Even without a house on the site, we trilled, we could pitch a tent here or park a caravan and the views alone would be enough to nourish our souls.

There was the vineyard immediately behind the house, a sweep of olive grove to the north, undulating meadows and woodland areas to the south and fields of sunflowers to the east. The air was clear and sweet, the soundtrack a medley of bird song. If the house was derelict and overgrown, the land on which it stood was pure perfection.

All of which just goes to prove that love at first sight is not to be trusted. Our hearts were very much in charge at the time, and although our heads seemed to be assuring us that it was the right place to choose and made good sense, time and experience showed us that it was not. Had we moved in as full-time residents, it may have been fine; but as part-timers, with the house left at the mercy of Italy's wildlife and weather for weeks on end, it was a mistake.

Casa Rosa was the wrong sort of property to fit into the way we planned to use it – or rather the way we did use it, because to say we planned would be to allow ourselves greater credit and foresight than we merited. The truth is that we fell into a pattern whereby we maintained our base in England and visited Italy as often as we could.

A view of the sunset from the terrace at Casa Rosa.

And from the same spot the following night. No two sunsets ever seemed to be identical but they were always awesome.

We did not really accept the error of our ways for some years and always tried to make the best of things but deep down we knew; for all the compensations of living at Casa Rosa, and there were indeed many, there were too many negatives for a pair of occasional visitors lacking the skills, time or energy to overcome all that the house threw at us. We should have bought a place in a town or village, keeping nature at arm's length and hoping that we could have coped with the urban irritations of barking dogs and squawking neighbours, even if that had meant sacrificing some of the joy of the landscape. We were always quietly amused when friends back in the UK kindly enquired whether we had enjoyed our latest Italian holiday. Did we feel rested and refreshed by our latest taste of *La Dolce Vita*? It became easier just to say yes, lovely, thank you, rather than explain that it had not been a holiday and, while parts of it had indeed been hugely enjoyable and certainly memorable, it had most certainly not been restful or refreshing. Try ordeal, we thought, or stress.

If Le Marche's wildlife (see 'The war with nature') had been a major cause of the problems that Casa Rosa threw at us, it was certainly not alone. Truth be told, though, we encountered most of the issues when we first arrived at the house after an absence of more than a couple of weeks. A pattern established itself early on in our ownership of the house: our visits tended to start badly, sometimes horribly, and improve during the course of our stay.

A field of sunflowers illuminates the view from one of our windows.

It would have helped enormously had we ever found a good, reliable local resident, willing and able to keep a watchful eye over the house in our absence: check it from time to time, nip problems in the bud, deal with any urgent repairs or maintenance that may be needed, perhaps even make some small preparations for our arrival. On odd occasions when friends did step in and help, it was wonderful to arrive knowing all would be well. But the house's remoteness and inaccessibility, as well as the reluctance of locals to lift a finger, even for payment, conspired against our hopes.

Electricity, or rather the sudden absence of it, was at the root of many of the problems at the house. All the cables came overground, of course, transported across vast distances by cables carried by pylons. But it was a flaky system at best. A flatulent butterfly half a mile away would sometimes be sufficient to cause an outage; on other occasions, hurricane-force winds would batter us but the electricity supply remained defiant and robust. In a way, the whole unpredictable business was a metaphor for Italy itself. Usually, when we arrived in the spring after having left the house through several months of a fierce winter, all the services would be working perfectly. Casa Rosa would be insect-free, dry and welcoming, with all services behaving beautifully. But during the rest of the year, especially in the summer months, our arrivals were frequently met with the electricity off, wildlife in command, and we would have to deal with the consequences.

One small bunch of grapes, from just one small branch of just one vine: the harvest had been vast, and while most of the grapes went to make wine, we couldn't resist picking the occasional bunch for our own consumption.

Arriving at the house was always a tense time. Even if our absence had only been for three or four weeks, there was every likelihood that the grass would be shoulder-high, the lofty bamboos would have been blown horizontal by a summer storm, making access to the front door difficult, and there would be sinister signs of out-of-control insect life. Opening the front door, we would reach for the light switch and breathe a sigh of relief if it worked. Often it didn't so we groped around for the trip switch and then approached the fridge and freezer to deal with the smelly, messy consequences.

A July visit in 2009 was especially memorable. First we had been delayed for a couple of hours at Stansted because the scheduled Ryanair plane had broken down; the airline's singular customer care policy meant that we spent an hour-and-a-half standing on a hot staircase at the boarding gate before the replacement aircraft was available. When we finally reached Casa Rosa on a hot, sultry evening, we found the whole place horribly affected by mould. There had evidently been a prolonged period of exceptionally hot weather and heavy rain and there had been insufficient ventilation in the house.

There followed several days of laundering just about everything that could be laundered, as well as cleaning furniture and belongings; even the laptop was mouldy. The operation was not helped by the intermittent failure of the washing machine to work properly, due to the damp in its nether regions. The brushcutter, urgently required because of the height of the vegetation around the house, stubbornly refused to start.

The big lesson we took from the whole ordeal was that we needed to provide some ventilation because, once the windows and shutters were closed, the place was almost vacuum-sealed. We bought a dehumidifier to leave on during our absence but the threat of power cuts made this a less than foolproof answer, so we took to leaving some windows open behind the closed shutters, enabling a small amount of air to get in. A combination of the dehumidifier and the window configuration solved the problem.

The contadini – tenant farmers – hard at work dealing with the grape harvest.

The house flung so many other things at us during our ownership. We had a few instances of the main waste pipes from the house to the septic tank becoming blocked; the pump that sent the water from an outside reservoir into the house would pack up from time to time; the boiler would go on the blink occasionally despite being regularly serviced; sections of our makeshift garden fence would be mysteriously flattened and twisted as if by some clumsy use of heavy machinery – the tractor-driving *contadini* would shake their heads in dismay and bewilderment . . .

One of the most dramatic events came after a stormy night. We went outside in the morning to discover that a brick had been tugged completely out of the front wall near the top of the house and had the main electricity connection attached to it. The cable was swinging in mid-air with the brick attached, at about neck height. We still had power but it was a perilous situation.

Desperate phone calls to Enel, the electricity company, ended in failure as we were unable to grasp the options offered at breakneck speed on the automated response, so we called an Italian friend, who phoned on our behalf. The Enel engineers duly arrived next morning with a long ladder, a bucket of cement, a beaming smile and fixed it. They didn't want the power switched off while they did it. There was no charge, no stress and they even took the trouble to re-hang a troublesome upstairs shutter for us while they were about it.

A brick carrying the main electricity cable into the house had been yanked out of the wall by the storm.

The men from the electricity company replace the brick.

The perils of flying

Falconara Airport, a few miles from Le Marche's main city, Ancona, had a pretty basic terminal building when we first landed there in 2001. During the years we regularly used it, they spent an awful lot of euros building a swish new terminal alongside the old one, larger, better equipped, with more room for shops and cafés and bags of space for uniformed Italian people to strut around.

The interior layout, however, was far more style than substance, with a woefully inadequate number of seats, dreadful acoustics, poorly thought-out design and a general air of chaos and panic of the kind that the Italians are so very good at. Lots of glass, lots of walking around and a distinct lack of comfort or logic.

Also absent from the upgrading work was the system that enables airports to continue their principal function – that of enabling aeroplanes to land and take off – when visibility is poor. Falconara, close to the Adriatic coast, is prone to fog but we discovered several times that it doesn't have to be a pea-souper to bring the airport to a shuddering halt: a very light mist or just the faintest haze will do the job just as effectively. We have on occasions stood looking across the runway in what seemed to our uninitiated eyes to be crystal clear conditions while being told that there would be no planes taking off from or landing at Falconara today because of fog. Most airports, apparently, have the technology to cope in even quite dense fog but not Falconara. Nice cafeteria, though. Great coffee.

The result, after several hours of waiting and being told absolutely nothing, is that a fleet of buses arrives, there is a free-for-all as overwrought passengers clamber on board, and then there follows a two-hour drive south to the Third World – or Pescara airport in Abruzzo, as it is known.

The last time this happened to us, the elderly coach driver was in a state of such nervous tension that we seriously doubted that we would make it in one piece; he needed two hands and all his strength to wrench the lever from one gear to another, and he could not find his way into the airport once we reached Pescara. We finally got home to Dorset ten hours behind schedule.

Fog at Ancona has also caused us to be diverted to Pescara when travelling from the UK. Needless to say, there was no bus fleet waiting to whisk us by road to Falconara. It seemed to come as quite a shock to the ground crew when three hundred people poured into the arrivals hall at Pescara airport. The buses came eventually and we all reached our cars or our lifts at Falconara five hours late.

Ryanair, of course, has over the years earned itself a dubious reputation for many reasons; it has become the Trabant of airlines. Actually, it would be more accurate to say it was the Skoda equivalent – once a laughing stock and the butt of many jokes but now a highly successful manufacturer with a prestigious badge. Ryanair is nothing like as bad as it is often portrayed, but poor reputations are notoriously difficult to live down.

If you have a house in central or southern Le Marche and want to fly to an airport somewhere within easy reach, then it has to be Ancona or Pescara and it has to be Ryanair. On the scores of occasions we have flown with Ryanair, we have found them generally to be reliable, punctual and good value. Since they brought in such world-shattering innovations as pre-booking of seats to avoid the stressful stampede at boarding time, we have found them to be perfectly acceptable.

What has been troublesome, though, has been the airline's occasional changes of schedule. When you choose an area in which to buy a property – in Italy, France, where ever – one of the main factors to take into account is accessibility. When we bought Casa Rosa, there were two flights daily into Ancona and at times that suited us. But there have been a number of changes since then and we are mighty glad we are no longer dependent on Ryanair's flight schedules. They're not the only airlines that do this, of course, as they all have to take account demand and profitability, but a sudden switch from a late morning flight to a late evening one can wreak havoc with holiday plans.

For travellers to Le Marche, if they don't like Ryanair for whatever reason, there are other airlines serving other destinations, such as Rome and Bologna, but they are all some hours away by road and may even necessitate overnight hotel stays on arrival, departure or both. It sure changes the rules and the costs.

We have had fights cancelled or delayed for several days because of air traffic control strikes in northern Italy or, more usually, France. We had our return to England delayed by five days on one occasion because of the volcanic vomit emanating from Iceland which paralysed air traffic across western Europe (see *Trapped under a cloud in paradise'* below); we have had long delays at Stansted because of what was described as security matters – once when some clown had left an unattended bag and another time when the number of bags aboard was one more than had been checked in so the alarm was raised and we spent two extra hours in the terminal building. Once, at Ancona, the queue for our flight was so long and so slow-moving that we really thought we would not make in on board; when we did, we found we were unable to sit together and there was no room for our luggage in the overhead cupboards. Rosie found herself next to the winner of Italy's fattest human being competition so she spent the flight folded in half.

Rosie wrote this in 2010 about being delayed by the Icelandic volcano:

Trapped under a cloud in paradise

Ah, so that's why nautical stripes are so fashionable this season. It's in case we find ourselves being piped aboard one of Her Majesty's warships, heading for home waters after being scooped up from a distant shore.

My striped jumper is to hand, my nautical phrases freshly honed and my anti-seasick wristbands are poppered into place. I'm ready, aye ready, to sing 'Heart of Oak'. I'm teetering on the edge of the gangplank to start my voyage home. I'm all yours, HMS Ark Royal, now get me back to Blighty. But where are you?

Nowhere round these parts, that's for sure. At the last count, what possibly amounts to the entire British naval fleet was destined to transform itself into a public ferry service, which is fine if you're a Brit in Spain but not all that helpful if, like David and me, you're a pair of Brits in Italy.

Yes, predictably, we are among the wandering tribes of lost Britons, sad folk stuck far from home at the mercy of That Cloud, the great smouldering rage of ash pitched up by the eruption of Iceland's unpronounceable, unspellable but forever memorable volcano.

We were due to fly back to sun-drenched Stansted this week after staying in the same place as last year, when we were affected by the terrible earthquake in L'Aquila.

We're beginning to think that Italy and April don't make the perfect combination for us. However, there are worse places to be stuck than a peaceful hillside looking out from the terrace across a vineyard green-spiked with new growth, with the Apennines beyond and the sparkling Adriatic Sea behind us. Yes, many worse places indeed, for this is not unlike some kind of paradise.

But even paradise can experience its little panic attacks. We're fairly relaxed about the delays to our flight and will go when the plane's ready and when someone has kindly air-brushed out all that dangerous mess from the sky. Farmer Luigi, in contrast, thinks this crisis of the skies is the beginning of the end.

He pauses in his hand-wringing just long enough to hand over a Sunday-lunch gift from his mamma Rosa of three lettuces, ten eggs and a still-warm, part-incinerated, mahogany-brown chicken with its head intact and secreted somewhere unmentionable. Believe me, as a non-meat eater, it takes a strong nerve not just to embrace such a thing but to carry on smiling and expressing gratitude while the donor is banging on about 'la crisi' and 'l'effetto domino' of airport closures.

I eventually manage to shove the contorted, wizened little bird into the fridge and concentrate on Luigi's torment. It turns out that, just like Giovanni who runs the toytown-sized village supermarket, he has a son who is trying to get to London to study. The earliest flight they can get on is May 17. So what's wrong with thumbing a lift, I joke, pointlessly. It falls very flat. The Italians prefer slapstick, I find. An English family with teenagers due to sit GCSE and A-level exams in north London resorted to the trains, travelling up half of Italy, into southern France, and then up to Calais where we last heard they were queuing for a ferry on Sunday night. Others have given up trying to rearrange their flights and are driving back, sharing cars where possible and being resourceful, as you'd expect battling Brits to be.

Meanwhile, the natives look up at the sky and do a bit more hand-wringing. Amazing, isn't it, how our whole so-called sophisticated way of life, with its inter-continental travel at supersonic speeds, can be brought to a sudden, devastating halt by the power of Nature. A great leveller, lava.

And this the following week:

Our bonus week ends with a guilt trip

When I wrote last week about being stranded abroad because of the cloud of volcanic ash, I said that there were worse places to be sitting it out than in the paradise of a peaceful rural hillside in Italy.

That was before the rains came. While the UK was bathed in sunshine last week, we sploshed around in wellies under lashing rain. 'Primavera' is such a pretty word for spring, but this was ugly stuff indeed and David and I felt particularly aggrieved that it was wrecking our unexpected bonus week.

Happily, though, as I write this, with our delayed flight home beckoning us all too soon, the sun has been beaming down again and we've forgiven it for abandoning us so heartlessly.

Sun on Sunday meant that traditional celebrations were able to be held to mark Italy's national Liberation Day, which commemorates the relief of the country by the Allies and the retreat of the Germans in 1945. These shenanigans take the form of festas and fairs and, especially, big village picnics like the ones they enjoy at Easter. Since this is the country that hardly needs any excuse to hold a celebration – there's even a festa of Nutella on the local calendar – a giant picnic is the perfect occasion as it features food by the ton, wine by the lake, and a heaven-sent opportunity to converse at the very highest volume and do a lot of hand-waving.

Organisation is minimal. Things just happen and it's all a big happy muddle. Children don't get endlessly entertained with face painting and other so-called 'fun activities' as in Britain but make their own entertainment – just as we did in our childhood. In some cases this involves simply staring at each other's ludicrous and unsuitable clothing while tethered to a parent's hand, or, in contrast, wild games of 'It' and sliding down slopes, getting into scrapes and sorting out differences without resort to a team of psycho-babbling counsellors from a Department of Spoilt Brats.

Liberation Day also marked the day that a massive herd of sheep found the freedom of new pastures, thanks to an annual pilgrimage of several miles on their curious stick-legged tip-toes, bells a-tinkling, along local roads and lanes. It was just our luck to meet them head on, so we pulled the car in to let them pass – and pass, and pass and pass. Hundreds and hundreds of them flowed by, shepherded by half-a-dozen giant white dogs that growled 'Out of my way, punk' in Italian dialect, and, of course, because this is Italy, a human shepherd gesticulating wildly with a mobile phone clamped to one ear.

Nutty though it was, that vignette came nowhere near the 'worryingly strange' category that merits collection in our anecdotes headed 'You Would Not Believe What Happened . . .'

But this next one did. I was in a café in the nearest big town the other day when I found myself next to a nun in a brown habit. She caught my eye and we smiled at each other. That was obviously all the encouragement she needed because she then started speaking to me.

With Italian as our common language, we introduced ourselves and she told me she came from Eritrea. I was amazed. I wanted to squeak at her that I'd never met anyone from Eritrea before but I didn't want to sound rude and launch into a load of nosy questions. Even so, she captivated me with her charming manner and I thought she was lovely.

After the protracted getting-to-know-you niceties were out of the way, she hit straight in with what I quickly presumed had motivated her approach: would I please help to get her brother released from prison in Manchester?

As favours go, that was a big one. I'm afraid my answer ended up as 'No', but only after I'd explained to her that my normal life is about as remote from Manchester and legal matters as hers is. That took some explaining, especially in Italian, my voice almost drowned out by the torrential rain outside. We parted friends, but I still feel a great sense of guilt – which may have been her real mission. Who knows?

Weather beaten

It's one of the first things the Brits mention when they're listing all the things they love about Italy. Ah, the Mediterranean climate, where the sun shines every day and life is lived outdoors. Except, of course, that it isn't. In our part of central Italy, the weather often flips between extremes: vicious cold and paralysing heat.

One of the worst aspects is the weather's unpredictability. We have sat in shirtsleeves on our terrace on Christmas Day enjoying the sun and a cloudless blue sky; we have spent much of June hunkered down with the central heating on as the cold rain hammered down for days on end.

In Le Marche winter reminds you it's on its way around early November when fog takes a leading role. Often, though, it can be well after the turn of the year before the most severe winter weather descends, and that can mean deep snow lasting for weeks.

A wintry scene in our vineyard but this was actually March.

In November of 2005, unusually early wintry weather that had engulfed much of Europe turned our last Casa Rosa visit of the year into an ordeal and wrecked our plans. The intention had been to fly out, spend a few days at the house and then drive our car back to the UK. In fact, a blizzard began as we approached Montottone, turning Via del Colle into a skidpan, so we spent barely ten minutes at the house, flung a few items into cases, and decided to attempt to ascend the hill before the snow got too deep. After an arduous and anxious battle against the elements, we finally reached the summit and spent a chilly night at the *pensione* before setting off for England the next morning.

Where Italian snow scores over its British equivalent, though, is that the air feels crisper and dryer, and when the sun breaks through, there is warmth enough to raise the spirits.

Casa Rosa shivers beneath two feet of snow. Fortunately we were not in residence at the time.

The main summer months of July and August are, usually, hot – far hotter than we ever encounter in England and often considerably hotter than is tolerable for normal activity. For holidaymakers seeking their annual tan, it can be wonderful; but if you are living there and need to shop, or queue or work, it's a case of sprinting between air-conditioned cars and offices. Casa Rosa was too modest a house to stretch to air-con so it hummed to the non-stop sound of fans located around the house.

Just a month after the snow, the vineyard is a mass of spring flowers.

We learned from experience that the English instinct to throw open windows when the weather is warm is not the brightest thing to do in extreme heat; the best option is to close the shutters against the sun, keep doors and windows closed and turn the fans to full speed. At night, with temperatures still uncomfortably hot and sticky, open the bedroom windows fully but be sure to keep the fly-screens in place or you'll find yourself knee-deep in brightly coloured moths before you know it. The hum of the fans should, with luck, drown out the sounds of barking dogs (*see below*).

When the weather finds its happy medium, though, Italy is truly perfect – but then much the same could be said of the UK, too. Spring and autumn are usually joyous times to be in Le Marche. But many times we have known communities cut off for days on end by waist-deep snow and on others it has been so savagely hot that we have confined ourselves to the house until late in the evening.

Dog days

Italian dogs are rather like Italian people – noisy, excitable, unpredictable and almost impossible to quieten. Barking dogs provide the most widespread soundtrack in rural Italy. Night and day, summer and winter, the all-pervasive noise of barking dogs sometimes seems to overwhelm everything.

The Italians' relationship with their dogs is hard to fathom. It's certainly very different from what we are accustomed to in England, where so many people adore their pets as much as they do their children and often more. They are part of the family. The Brits take them shopping, on outings to the country or the beach, they take them for walks. They speak to them and stroke them and hug them. Sometimes they even train them.

It's not like that in Italy. Many people have dogs but we have often wondered why. They rarely seem to show affection for their dogs or even take much notice of them at all. In the rural areas of Le Marche, many bigger animals are kept as guard dogs while the little ones act as intruder alarms.

The sounds of big dogs barking and small dogs yapping echo across the valleys of Le Marche almost constantly, and while it makes foreigners want to scream in frustration or go and buy a shotgun to silence the canine hordes, the Italians simply don't appear to hear them. We have stood outside Cristina's house chatting with her while her two dogs have circled us at high speed, just a few feet away, bouncing up and down repeatedly and barking themselves into a state of nervous breakdown and yet she did nothing to silence them until she noticed us rolling on the ground screaming and clutching our ears.

In our little house on the hillside, the barking was bad enough, booming across the valleys from the hilltop roads far away. But in the centre of the village itself, it could be worse. Often we have walked around its narrow, ancient streets, invariably whisper-quiet as so many Italian villages tend to be, and suddenly there would be an explosion of noise as some monstrous creature hurled itself at a gate or fence as we walked past. It sounded as though it was the size of a bear and it always had us trembling with the shock of it and thanking heaven that we did not have a house nearby.

Driven to distraction

Italians love their cars. They will never walk even a short distance when it is possible to drive. Fifty yards to the shop? Crank up the Fiat. Sun, rain or sleet, the Italians will always take the car option if they possibly can.

There are, in our experience, two distinct types of Italian drivers. The better-known one – let's call him Fabrizio – has the skill of Lewis Hamilton. However, Fabrizio drives slightly faster than the Formula One ace. He does it not on racetracks but on motorways, minor roads, village streets, petrol station forecourts and even in his front drive.

Fabrizio drives like that while holding the steering wheel between his knees. His hands are being used for more important functions, like clutching his mobile phone, gesticulating to whoever is on the other end of the phone call, lighting his cigarette, forking ravioli into his mouth, or reading a newspaper. Or he might be fondling Mara alongside him.

Fabrizio will be doing some or all of these things, at close to the speed of light, while using a bit of an elbow to flash his headlights to encourage the driver of the car one micro-millimetre ahead of him to get the hell out of his way so that he can chase down Jensen Button before the next turn-off on the autostrada.

Fabrizio pilots a big German job and it will almost certainly be silver. If not, it will be black. But it will be moving so quickly that it could just as well be a Harrier Jump Jet in blushing pink metallic. If Fabrizio ever comes to the UK and drives in his normal fashion, he will not have travelled far before he learns all sorts of quaint English expressions and customs. New phrases will boost his vocabulary, such as 'road rage' and 'smack inda mouth' and 'you're nicked, old son, and no, you can't phone your mama'.

In certain parts of Italy, it is even more terrifying. Naples is a nightmare but experience has taught us that Sicily is probably the worst. Its capital, Palermo, warrants a chapter to itself but I can't find the adjectives to do it full justice.

This is an article I wrote in 2005:

Sicily: where driving is a blood sport

It is a miracle that any Sicilian survives into middle age. It is as if every mad, bad, reckless driver on the face of the planet has been rounded up and compelled to spend their days on the island's twisty roads.

They drive at speeds more suited to Monza and in vehicles that look quite incapable of reaching such speeds, battered and bruised by countless contretemps. They are usually elderly Fiats, although some vehicles better resemble kitchen implements or household gadgets.

Most Sicilians drive attached to your rear bumper, filling your rear view mirror like some cartoon monster. They resemble a sexually aroused dog trying to mount a timid fleeing bitch on heat. They drive glued to your boot. A one-inch gap between vehicles is for wimps or foreigners. Half their car is across the centre of the road so that if a gap longer than six feet or one millisecond should present itself, they can screech past, scaring the wits out of their unwary victim and forcing oncoming vehicles to swerve into the verge.

Yet it rarely provokes anger because it is routine. In the UK, where road rage thrives, the average Sicilian driver would be lucky indeed to reach the end of the road before being ambushed and beaten to a pulp.

They race up to junctions where they are supposed to give way and don't. They nudge a yard or more out into the road, convincing you that they are going to pull straight out. Sometimes they do, but usually it is just a challenge to the mental fortitude of the oncoming driver to see if he hits his brakes. If he does, the Sicilian driver pulls straight out and vanishes into the distance like some earthbound UFO. The knack is to brace yourself, convince yourself that, no, they wouldn't, and carry on. Usually you survive that way and they overtake you one second later.

Scenes of accidents are more common on the roads than lay-bys; the sound of sirens from ambulances dashing, recklessly, towards crash scenes is a familiar soundtrack. In the most narrow and serpentine of country lanes, it is common to round a corner and find two cars buried into one another smack in the centre of the carriageway while two bewildered drivers stand discussing it and wondering how they could have been so unlucky.

Speak to any Sicilian and they agree that the driving is appalling. Yet nothing changes. Sicily had me trembling like a leaf in the wind within seconds of picking up the hire car; calculating, before every trip, whether it perhaps it might not be nicer to walk. It had me going out feeling like a soldier off to war and returning as if having survived one.

They overtake on the narrowest of roads going almost vertically up or down cliffs. Now and then we saw manoeuvres so unbelievable in their conception and breathtaking in their execution that they must surely have been learnt in a circus. Any moment a door would drop off, perhaps, or a comical horn honk? A motorist would leap out wearing yard-long shoes and a shiny red nose? But no, just an ordinary day on any Sicilian road.

The second species of Italian driver – we'll call him Peppe – comes from a different planet from Fabrizio and inhabits a different time zone. In Peppe's murky, quiet world, absolutely nothing moves quickly. Peppe will be crushed behind the wheel of something that no scrappage scheme would accept. It may be a pock-marked rusting Lancia from the early Jurassic period or an old Vespa with a third wheel, a dog-cart string-tied to its back end and piled high with turnips, and the forward thrust of an egg-whisk.

Absolutely nothing would tempt Peppe to speed up from a relaxed walking pace, even supposing his time machine was capable of acceleration. He lives his life and makes his journeys oblivious to all that is going on in the world beyond those rusting doors. Peppe is sometimes seen on the autostrada but he will probably be lost or asleep; his natural domain is Italy's spaghetti of twisting lanes and village streets where the locals know that he is myopic, stone deaf, a hundred years old and with no brakes or teeth. There is no danger of Peppe ever coming to England because he has rarely ventured from his village. He's heard of England, but then he's heard of Mars, too, and he's not likely to visit.

So visit Italy at your own risk but be very wary of the locals. Fabrizio will introduce himself to you before you get the hire car into second. Peppe will be lying in wait. You have been warned.

Television torment

Spend an evening or two watching Italian television and I guarantee you will never again grumble about the fare served up on British screens.

The mainstream Italian channels are dominated by puerile game shows, grimly reminiscent of British programmes of the Seventies or even earlier but, of course, with the most convoluted rules. Typically they would be a perfect reflection of Italy's overtly sexist attitude: presented by a smug-looking middle-aged man sporting what looks at first like a cheap toupee but is probably his own carefully coiffured and dyed hair. He, all flashing smile and smooth patter, is assisted by a bevy of scantily clad, pouting girls, with legs up to their ear lobes, come-hither leers and enough lip-gloss to use as a mirror.

To describe the humour as unsophisticated would be an understatement. There is absolutely no place for subtlety in Italian TV humour; slapstick is king and nothing draws a laugh from an Italian audience quite like someone falling over – unless it's someone falling over and all their clothes coming off.

The general air of bewilderment is compounded because, at any given moment, the show presenters may pop up to endorse some commercial product made by the programme sponsor. Is it an advertisement break or just a brief aside to fill a gap between the thigh-slapping laughter and fun of the show? It's hard to be sure.

Almost the ultimate insult imposed by the TV channel's bean counters comes in a football match when a corner kick is being lined up and the picture rapidly switches to a packet of breakfast cereal or floor cleaner. It is an act of sacrilege that only a football fan would fully understand, and made all the worse when the picture flicks back to the game in time to see the attacking team celebrating a goal. And this in a country where they delight in calling *calcio* – football – a religion.

The news and magazine programmes are relatively well done, once your eyes get accustomed to the clothing and make-up of the presenters. The weather forecasters often appear in uniform, complete with coloured braid, but our initial assumption that this was due to the Italians' predilection for dressing up was corrected when we discovered that the presenters were, in fact, members of the Italian Air Force. That also probably explained why we generally found the forecasts far more accurate and reliable than we Brits are accustomed to.

Italians seem obsessed with televisions, addicted to them. They feature large in restaurants. In Italy, certainly in the rural areas of Le Marche and elsewhere, most restaurants bear no resemblance whatever to the romanticised British version of an Italian restaurant, with its subtle lighting, soft atmospheric background music, checked tablecloths and flirtatious waiters. In Italy they have harsh overhead lighting and booming television sets with massive screens, often several scattered around the place and sometimes tuned to different channels. There is usually no escape.

We have eaten at the homes of Italian friends when there is no talking at meal times because the whole family are staring at their television. Sometimes they will rock with laughing approval at the sort of slapstick mishap that you might expect on CBeebies for under-fives. The television set remains, even in the 21st century, something of a status symbol in Italy. The nation is utterly hooked and the quality dreadful.

Here's a piece that Rosie wrote as we neared the end of a visit to Casa Rosa in 2009:

A sad farewell to all this madness

All good things come to an end, and so by the time you read this David and I will have turned our backs on our Italian idyll and returned to Dorset.

At least we're not going back to some fume-filled industrial city, David keeps saying, trying to encourage me out of the gloomy pits where I descend whenever I think of not being here on this dramatically beautiful hillside any more. Then there's the homeward journey and all that it involves. Airports, for a start, which are only a cattle prod away from being complete replicas of livestock markets, and the M25 and M3, where progress is entirely in the hands of Fate since we could be at walking speed or 70mph.

Anyway, that's all for another day, thank goodness. Before then I want to linger and soak up what remains for me here in Italy, stretching out the final days and locking into my memory all the huggable, wonderful and nutty things that make this country so incomparably endearing.

Unconditional love, such as I have for Italy, means severe shortcomings in many areas have to be tolerated. One of these is the abysmal standard of television where, for example, simpering, dirigible women presenters dressed in little more than a plunging neckline are teamed with lascivious men of an orange hue. Unsurprisingly, the overall impression is of glitter and no substance. Contrast that with the weather forecasters, who you would expect to be completely naked as they announce another day of blistering heat. No, because this is Italy and because it is a curious country of perpetual enigmas, they appear in serge uniforms bristling with gold braid and shirts secured at the neck with a sombre tie.

I went to the market in the village this morning. I wanted some vegetables but, after assessing the situation, feared I might not live long enough to get served, since the queue that had built up around signora's trestle table at the back of her van looked as though it would still be there come next market day. Each time a customer asked for something that she didn't have among the half-dozen items displayed, she would hitch her dress up to reveal a fine pair of Norah Batty-style stockings and, with much clatter and commotion, clamber into the depths of the van to fetch it.

Nobody minded signora's painful and painfully slow method of serving her customers. She'd no doubt been doing it that way for years, and anyway the long wait meant everyone could exchange gossip and chatter to their hearts' content. And that, of course, is what it is all about. Fresh food, served slowly, with time to talk and think and appreciate the fruits of the earth. Big, dew-damp Romana lettuces grown just down the road being lugged out of a box in the back of a battered old van. Picked this morning, bought this morning, eaten at lunchtime. Slow, slow food indeed.

And then you drive somewhere and find there isn't much that's slow about Italy when the men get behind the wheel of a car. Whoosh – some maniac's gone past us at the speed of light and we're bound to find him dead in the road round the next corner. No? Well, he made it – this time. We, of course, come over all of a sweat, stunned that people who can spend six hours having lunch will then try and get home before they've even left.

See, I said it's a nutty place. Nutty but nice. Very, very nice.

The neighbours

In any country, bad neighbours can make your life a misery and good ones a joy. We and the various ex-pats with whom we formed friendships during our years in Le Marche had mixed fortunes.

At Casa Rosa, at the end of a white road, we had only one neighbouring house and we were fortunate that Cristina brought only positivity to our lives in Italy. She divided her time between her appealingly shambolic house and garden, where she grew much of her own fruit and vegetables and kept a few pigeons for meat days, and her little studio – which she referred to as her laboratory – in the village where she produced ceramics to sell at markets and fairs around the region.

Cristina was wise in the ways of the countryside, knowing which weeds to collect for cooking, and understanding the vagaries of the Italian climate. While she lived simply and seemed to shun many of the trappings of modern Italian life, she was an intelligent, educated woman. Her living-room was lined with shelves groaning with books – something we seldom encountered in Italy – and she had, for us, the great bonus of being a fluent English speaker. That talent rescued us countless times, especially in our early years in the country when the language was just one of the things that reduced us to a state of flustered confusion.

We developed a good balance in our relationship with Cristina. We would, once in a while, eat at one another's houses, and we both knew that we would be happy to help out in any way we could, but there was enough distance between us, in all senses, for us to live independently and privately.

Some of our friends in Le Marche were less fortunate.

It has become a widespread tendency in recent years for many rural-dwelling Italians with more land than cash to build themselves a new home adjacent to their old one. Invariably the new one will be *brutto* - ugly – but spacious enough to swallow up two or three generations of the family. Then they put the old house up for sale, knowing that foreigners will be captivated enough by its charm to renovate it or sufficiently enticed by its panoramic location to demolish it and build anew. If the vendors have built a respectful distance from the old house, that has tended to work out to everyone's satisfaction, but some have built so close by that their proximity becomes a deterrent and the plan has failed. The old house gets abandoned to nature or the family's hens.

One British couple with whom we became quite friendly, mainly as a result of chatting at restaurants or in airport queues, bought just such an old house in a hamlet a few miles from Montottone. We could never quite understand what it was about it that snared them because its location was unspectacular and the house was in a dire state. Anyway they bought it.

The actual restoration project turned into a full-scale nightmare – the difficult site location, seriously dishonest and/or incompetent builders, a disinterested *geometra*, escalating costs, a time scale that slipped from months to years – and the whole process was further compounded by the neighbours.

The original Italian owners lived in their new house next door for a while and all was *tranquillo*. Then the Italians sold – to a huge family of Romanians, whose numbers were swelled by their ownership of half a dozen big, aggressive, noisy dogs. The new neighbours were loud, inconsiderate, unfriendly, everything you'd want them not to be, and the dogs were a hideous and constant presence, wandering unrestricted.

Our friends, also pummelled by family problems back home in England, running short of money and with their own mental and physical health deteriorating, were at their wits' end. The last time we saw them, they were on the point of just walking away and putting the house on the market. Of course, by then, property values in the area were collapsing in the face of the global economic recession – and that was before Brexit and a series of central Italian earthquakes piled on more misery.

Another couple of our acquaintance moved from London to Le Marche to restore a large old property and transform it in to an upmarket B&B. They made a beautiful job of it and, although hard work, it was very successful. Now and then one of them would pop back to England for family reasons or to check on their London flat and life was all they had hoped it would be.

Then one day, out of the blue, a letter arrived threatening legal action because a very small part of the grassy driveway leading from the road to their property allegedly cut across a few feet of a neighbour's land. They had never heard a whisper of a problem but felt sure that, if that was the case, they could come to an amicable arrangement with the neighbour.

Needless to say, they couldn't. A dispute blew up involving lawyers, surveyors, planners and nearby residents; it dragged on for years, and cost the B&B couple their health and many thousands of euros. I don't know how it was resolved or even if it was resolved but it was a graphic example of just how drastically an unpleasant, unreasonable and uncaring neighbour can affect your life.

Open for business?

Summertime visitors to Italy quickly see the logic of most shops being closed for much of the afternoon. The sometimes fierce heat makes working and shopping uncomfortable so the three or four hours of siesta makes perfect sense. Lock up at lunchtime – maybe midday or 1pm – then spend the afternoon having a snooze somewhere before reopening for business in the early evening. It can be a little frustrating for an ex-pat needing to buy something but, hey, that's the way it works so you have to get used to it.

What doesn't make so much sense, though, is that the same rules apply in the winter, too. An afternoon nap is the last thing people need when there's snow on the ground and the temperature is several degrees below freezing. Why close the premises for four or five hours, only to reopen well after dark until mid-evening when the cars are all iced solid and most sensible people are at home watching fifth-rate game shows on TV?

Not all shops and businesses operate the same sort of opening routines, however. Many places, especially restaurants, don't open at all on Mondays, for instance; our bank branch opened for only forty-minutes in the afternoon, and with the slowness of the service and the length of the queues, it really wasn't worth your while visiting. One hair salon we knew had a hand-scrawled sign on its door saying it only opened for fifteen minutes twice a week.

It took us a long time to get to grips with the shop hours in Le Marche. If we made a slow start to the day – as we usually did – it was often late morning before we had decided what we needed to buy from the ironmongers or electrical store or whatever – but we knew there would be queues, and would probably close for lunch before we reached the front, so it was probably best to stay home and venture out when they reopened at four o'clock. Unless it was the third Wednesday after a full moon in Gemini and happened to be Saint Federico's Day, in which case they wouldn't be reopening until Saturday fortnight. Obviously. Actually saints' days seem to happen with astonishing frequency in Italy, so it's usually a sensible plan to avoid trying to shop or eat out or do anything much on a Monday.

Village events

The Italians love a festival and the villages stage them in honour of almost every food or drink item you can think of. In our time in Le Marche, we attended, among others, celebrations of wheat, watermelons, Carlsberg and even Nutella, a real Italian favourite.

In our village, Montottone, the annual *festa* stretched to two full weeks and if the various events changed little from year to year, they were no less enjoyable for that. There was a celebration with music and dancing in the main piazza, where *vincisgrassi*, a local variant of lasagne, was served. It was washed down with locally produced young red wine or water in paper cups, and it was truly wonderful. We would see all the same, familiar faces at every event. Some people would greet us like long-lost family, others would stare as though we were horned invaders from the planet Zog.

The Montottone *festa* included an extraordinary parade of tractors, mostly ancient, chugging beasts displayed and driven with immense pride by ancient, chugging owners. Tractors and drivers alike would all gather in the piazza, hooting, coughing and occasionally backfiring, before setting off on a long, slow procession around the village, finishing with a static display outside the *oleficio*, the olive oil depot, which would be the location for that evening's fun. That took the form of a live band performing on the *oleficio* forecourt while the villagers danced and flirted and ate and drank. The night ended with a firework display.

Tractors take pride of place in the piazza during one of Montottone's festa events.

On another night during the festa, we enjoyed, or endured, a rock band competition, the boom of electric guitars and amplified singers bouncing off the village's ancient walls. Another evening we went along to an accordion concert in one of the small squares, where, at one in the morning, we bumped into the mayor and nagged for the thousandth time for some repair work to be done on our road. One night there was a watermelon festival and on yet another, gnocchi was the star turn on the menu. We decided to give the Nutella and Carlsberg events a miss.

Arguably the most extraordinary event that we witnessed in Montottone was a *palio*. To say it was a far cry from the famous Siena *palio*, in which heroic men gallop on horses around the vast *campo*, urged on by thousands of spectators, would be something of an understatement. Rosie wrote a column about it at the time in 2013 and I reproduce it here:

Balmy nights and coloured tights

Italian communities need little excuse to stage a celebration. They turn on the party mood for anything from saints to squid, from sausages to shrimps.

Our village has been having a high old time paying homage in various ways to the saints associated with its five churches - yes, five, in a village of 1,000 souls. There has been food, lots of it, enjoyed at trestle tables under the stars in the piazza, music, dancing, a volleyball tournament and a solemn procession up and down the hills around the village stopping at each church, accompanied by the oompah band, a tolling bell and an occasional exploding firework.

Prominent in the parade was a huge gold-framed portrait of the Madonna, topped with a crown and carried shoulder-high on a red velvet bier by a team of strong men. Along the route, gold-trimmed red cloths hung from windows as a mark of respect.

After more fireworks and the release into the velvet sky of scores of coloured lanterns there was a big shared meal in the piazza, by which time it was about 11pm and not one child was tucked up in bed. All were happy participants in a timeless, deeply affecting event that drew the little community together to confirm its faith and say a God-fearing thankyou to the saints.

The previous week the mood had been very different when a palio was held in the medieval centre of the village to decide the champion contrada, or neighbourhood. Unlike the famous palio in Siena, our men wore not dazzling racing silks but coloured tights. And there were no horses.

It was late, we'd all been eating for hours, the atmosphere was benign, the night was warm - but this was serious, there was a contest to win and glory to be had. David and I joined the crowds lining the cobbled street and waited to cheer our contrada, whose main man, Luigi, was in white tights and a velvet Renaissance-dude tunic instead of his usual farmer's overalls. As he is our very own contadino, we felt inordinately proud and proprietorial.

Each of the seven teams took it in turns to pull a racing sulky at speed along the cobbles. Bouncing unsteadily aboard the sulky was a man - Luigi was ours - holding a long lance with which to hit a thing like a giant saucepan suspended 15 feet up in the air as he passed underneath. A flag, white or red, held by a disembodied hand then appeared from an upstairs window to indicate if the hit had been fair or foul.

It was not gripping stuff, as David's weary expression made clear. The only real excitement came when one of the lances whacked the saucepan so hard it whizzed off-centre and had to be re-positioned. For this, a gang of volunteers in yellow, pink and turquoise tights held a ladder vertically while another in white tights clambered up and down to make adjustments. The operation, no doubt contravening every health and safety rule that bureaucracy could ever dream up, took us beyond midnight.

It was all very odd, very Italian and therefore completely unfathomable. But Luigi and our contrada won, so we can hold our head high as proud champions, of a sort.

Most of Montottone's population seemed to have turned out either to take part or to watch the fun and games that accompanied the palio.

Members of the triumphant palio team from our contrada, Eschito, including farmer Luigi and occasional restaurant waitress Mara.

An accordion player and friends were among the throng at a chestnut festival held in the nearby village of Belmonte Piceno.

An outdoor concert by the Montottone village band also featured in one of Rosie's columns in 2008:

In a hot spot and loving it

Under a deep blue velvet sky hung with the skinniest sliver of a new moon, David and I indulged in a dose of holiday culture on Sunday. We're in Italy at the moment, for the umpteenth time, being far too unadventurous to go anywhere other than the place we know and love best. Not for us, though, the delights of open-air opera – even though we're not far from one of the biggest and best venues. That's for another day, when we've saved up some more euros.

For this culture shot we sloped off after a delicious supper at the village restaurant down to the ancient piazza to find the village band in full swing. They were playing a selection of melodies in a programme that ranged from classical pieces to something unrecognisable by Elton John, of all people. Strange to find him represented here, in this remote outpost of rural Italy, far from the bright lights and glamour of his normal milieu.

Along with most of the rest of the village we sweated gently, and no doubt in several cases not quite so gently, on white plastic chairs (how the Italians love those hideous beasts) and wished we'd got there early enough to nab a place among the few rows of more forgiving wooden benches.

As at all such public gatherings the world over, a busy fringe of small children occupied themselves in earnest but silent games of death or glory, somehow finding the energy for physical exertion even though the clock neared midnight and the temperature was in the 30s.

For our part we sat motionless, a mixture of tiredness, excessive heat and admiration ensuring we stuck to our seats to the very end. Eventually, after successfully separating our damp behinds from their plastic prisons, we stood for the national anthem, as you do. Except of course it was their anthem not ours, which gives one a strange feeling.

We'd been pleased to recognise a few familiar faces among the band and the audience, people we've been served by in the village shop (sitting two rows in front of us), chatted with in the bar (clarinet), been served petrol by (trumpet) and seen in the bank (timpani). The band leader, we were intrigued to note, was none other than the man who combines his duties as deputy mayor with those of village barber and undertaker. I don't think he makes pies as well, but he'd give Sweeney Todd a run for his money, I'm sure.

And so, replete not just with good Italian food and wine but with this charming dose of culture too, we went back to the house, anticipating sleep, in my case with some relief, and in weary David's with something approaching desperation. He'd had to be elbowed sharply a few times during the concert each time a drooping eyelid snapped shut, so an accelerated trip bed-wards was imperative.

Nothing ever goes smoothly under these circumstances, does it? This being hot, hot Italy we first had to do battle with various uninvited guests: two very excitable crickets in the kitchen, a small scorpion on the sitting-room wall, a dragonfly, of all things, in the bedroom, and surely the world's biggest centipede, a full eight inches in length, on the bathroom floor.

After removing the zoo out into the garden, getting off to sleep in what seemed like a sauna set on extra high was a doddle. I know it may sound a bit masochist, but I am so pleased to think we have another week yet in this madly overheated corner of paradise. I just wish someone could find the 'medium' button.

A slightly bizarre sight at a festival of wheat at nearby Petritoli.

Another captivating village event we witnessed was a classic car cavalcade, organised in the nearby little town of Servigliano as part of the 2011 Republic Day celebrations. I reproduce here a column that I wrote at the time:

A car parade Italian style

While in Italy selflessly carrying out my study of Italian drivers and driving, I chanced upon an advertisement for a classic car parade being held as part of a village carnival. It was too good an opportunity to miss.

Rather like the driving – not to mention the food, the weather, the wine, the lifestyle, their World Cup record and almost everything else – it was very different from the sort of thing we know here in Britain.

It was billed to start at 10am. By 10.30am, two cars had arrived. They were both 1952 Fiats, one a snazzy sports convertible, the other a big, comfortable saloon. The gathered crowd spared them barely as glance but carried on chattering, milling about, buying things from stalls or watching the dressed-up ones emerge from Sunday morning church.

Around 11am, two more cars rolled up and were not so much parked as abandoned, keys in ignition and doors unlocked, while their owners strolled off to a nearby coffee bar. Around 11.30pm, there was a sudden cacophony of revving and squawking as another two dozen cars arrived together.

All the cars were then driven into a street just off the main square and parked with their noses tight against the high walls of the buildings, making it impossible for the now-interested onlookers to see anything other than the rear ends of the cars.

The vehicles themselves were a motley collection, dominated by Fiats, with a couple of Lancias, and a curiosity called an Autobianchi (a 1950s experiment involving a tie-up between Fiat, Bianchi and Pirelli) thrown in. Many were models I had never suspected existed, weird and wonderful, plus a few gorgeous red sporty Alfas looking much at home under the Italian sun. But here's an odd thing – most of the cars were grubby: unwashed, unpolished but evidently not unloved.

And what a motley crew the owners were too: a tiny, ancient, lipstick pink Fiat 500 disgorged a truly gigantic man – eventually – in a clashing scarlet sweater stretched taut across a vast stomach; an elderly Lancia was inhabited by a chaotic, arguing family, complete with yapping terrier. Concours d'Elégance it was not.

Then it was time for the cavalcade to hit the road and it did so in classic Italian style. All the cars had been parked Le Mans-fashion, facing the wall at an angle. The obvious way to leave would have been for them to depart in the same order as they had arrived.

But this was Italy; they all got into their vehicles simultaneously, they all hit reverse and total madness ensued: horns sounded, voices were raised, engines roared and revved as these enthusiasts' proudest possessions came within millimetres of smashing great dents into one another in their determination to get going.

It was an unchoreographed dance of the daft. A departure that, with a shred of common sense could have been completed smoothly within three or four minutes, had kept us rapt and open-mouthed for twenty.

Nobody made a fuss, nobody made unkind remarks, peace returned to the village square and the visitors quietly carried on milling, sipping their coffees and watching their Sunday-dressed offspring do precisely whatever they wanted.

A classic car gathering at Servigliano.

Ah, the food

You can get a lot of things in Italy – lost, confused, frustrated – but one thing that is very hard to get is a bad meal. I haven't dared to try and work out how many times we have eaten in restaurants in Italy but I know that I could count on the fingers of one hand the number of mediocre or poor meals we have experienced.

In the smartest of big-city restaurants or the most modest of village cafes, in friends' houses or in *autostrada* service stations, you can pretty well guarantee that the food will be terrific. The Italians do indeed pride themselves on their food; to borrow a well-worn cliché: the British eat to live, while the Italians live to eat.

Food plays a leading role in Italian life. So many of our friends there start planning the day's meals early: shopping at the market, preparing the ingredients in good time, always knowing what the evening's meal will be. Back home supper time arrives and we look in the fridge to see what lurks therein; it's very different in Italy, even for Brits who soon buy into the food culture.

They take great care over the quality of their ingredients, and locally grown or reared produce usually takes priority. Many people in the country set aside a patch of their land for an *orto* – a small allotment area – and when you see how expensive fruit and vegetables can be in the shops, it is small wonder they are prepared to make the effort to grow their own.

Restaurants exist in even quite small villages in our part of Le Marche and all seem to do a reasonable trade; friendly places, often with larger-than-life owners, they are usually noisy, harshly lit and dominated by massive television screens, but the food is almost invariably very good. The selection is limited very much by what is in season and what is obtainable locally. We have been told on a number of occasions that unfortunately the chicken or lamb is not local – the chef has had to travel three miles to the next village to obtain it. In the UK, we get it from New Zealand or Argentina.

Many of our happiest memories from our Italian years involve eating with friends – sometimes in favourite restaurants but more often around someone's huge table in the kitchen or, even better, outside on a terrace, surrounded by fragrant shrubs and fruit trees and a lot of laughter and good cheer. Magical times, enhanced by balmy evening temperatures.

Lunch on the terrace.

Many older Italians bemoan the decline of traditional home cooking as so many younger people fall under the spell of the fast-food industry, but I am happy to say that the only McDonalds within twenty miles of our village always seemed to be virtually empty. Those in Venice or Rome may be doing good business but in easy-paced Le Marche, pasta pummels burgers every day of the week.

The Italians are creatures of habit in so many aspects of their lives, but nowhere more than in their food choices. A meal without pasta is not a meal. It is rare to encounter an Italian prepared to entertain the concept of eating something different – British-style meat and two veg is anathema and heaven forfend trying anything as foreign as curry or Chinese food.

When Italian friends have visited us in England, they were keen – or they said they were keen - to try indigenous food; they were, to a man, convinced that we existed on nothing more than fish and chips and roast beef. Yet when we bought them fish and chips, they could not disguise their horror at the sight and taste.

The Italian preference for same old, same old is evidenced by what is on offer at the many small restaurants around our part of Le Marche. The menu (usually chanted ritualistically by the waitress or chef and very rarely written) was pretty much the same every single day, the only small differences coming when a particular ingredient came into or went out of season. But never, ever, anything completely new or, God forbid, exotic.

Our Italian village restaurant has remained a particular favourite over the years and is very typical. It is rarely less than moderately busy and sometimes, when there is a special event or a family celebration, it is absolutely rammed. On an average evening, there are all sorts of diners: families, couples, single-sex groups, solo diners. There will be workmen, still in their overalls, and there will be smartly dressed gatherings, and they will all be treated with friendly courtesy and they will all be respectful in their behaviour and the volume of their chatter.

One thing that struck us, from our very first visit back in 2001, was the choice of food - not that the selection was especially wide. Many is the time we have seen a group of maybe three or four men, grimy and dishevelled after a morning or a day of manual work nearby, enjoy a fresh green salad with their meal; it would be close to unthinkable in England. Typically the Italian workers' meal would also comprise a bowl of pasta, followed by a piece of meat and afterwards the vegetables. It would usually be washed down with water.

We learnt early on that it was by no means obligatory to order all the courses when going for a restaurant meal. At the very start of our Italian adventure, we well-mannered Brits followed what we thought to be the rule and ate ourselves into a bloated stupor, so finding that it was quite acceptable to eat more modestly saved us from a rapid journey into morbid obesity.

Rosie wrote this piece in 2004:

A world away from everyday life

I went to buy some vegetables this morning because I wanted to make soup for lunch. Sara in the shop wouldn't let me pay for the knobbly mis-shapen, half-green, half-red tomatoes. 'You have them as a present,' she said, 'because they've been in the shop for two days.'

The same went for the slightly bendy celery, which still had earth on its bottom and had probably been out of the ground for half the time of any of its plastic-bagged relatives in supermarkets.

Monday isn't the best day for catching the freshest of food at Sara's little shop, but if it's destined for the stockpot, then it's perfectly good enough. Two potatoes, an onion and some garlic were in better fettle, but I'd have to manage without courgettes as the neighbour in the village who supplies them couldn't deliver until the afternoon. Veggies safely stowed in my bag, I couldn't resist the display of fruit, especially since the peaches, Sara told me, came from a garden just down the road, and the watermelon had travelled only a little further, from a farm where they sell them at the gate for 30p apiece. Unpacking my bounty back at the house, I found Sara had secreted a slab of home-made cake in my shopping bag.

It's like that when you shop for food in Italy, especially in this dreamy rural backwater of Montottone. The fact that the sun is shining, the birds are singing their little hearts out, the butterflies are flitting and dancing like multi-coloured fairies and the only intrusive sound is an occasional clanking tractor across the valley, turns this longed-for holiday into something not far short of paradise.

Just to keep a tenuous hold on reality, I telephoned my daughter. I pushed the sunhat back off my head so that I could get the full benefit of her answer when I asked what the weather was like in England. I didn't want to miss one tiny detail of the rain, the weak sun, the grey clouds. 'Oh, poor you,' I said, as I gazed out across the shimmering countryside, and then I turned the knife a little more by recounting every mouthful, every morsel, of the amazing meal we'd enjoyed in a restaurant the night before. Cruel, I know, but sometimes having a heartless old bag for a mother can really help a girl grow up.

The amazing meal had included a selection of cheeses all made on the premises. We knew this as the young man of the house had given a graphic demonstration of hand-milking his cows and goats. His pride in their delicious products was matched by our pleasure in eating them, which, of course, prompted David and me to bemoan the state of affairs in the UK. I know it is possible to buy local cheeses, and we frequently do just that, but finding them on menus is a rarity and finding them in shops (by which I mean supermarkets, because proper grocery stores no longer seem to exist) is unheard of in my experience.

Though it pains me to recall it, as I sit here smugly under a glorious Italian sun, six months ago I asked in Tesco for a local cheese. I was offered a disinterested shrug and a slab of Wensleydale. I nearly wept.

Bambini

No-one indulges children quite like the Italians. They are with children as the English are with pets. They adore their offspring and are prepared to tolerate absolutely any level of misbehaviour. The children, needless to say, take full advantage and revel in being spoiled rotten. Other adults admire the children, even when there is really precious little to admire, but family is all-important to Italians.

Restaurants are among the children's favourite playgrounds. So often we have sat and tried to enjoy a quietish meal only to find ourselves under siege by one or two or sometimes complete hordes of children, running amok among the diners' tables, causing long-suffering waiters or waitresses to swerve around them; the faster and louder the brats behave, the more their parents smile with pride. Even when I have taken a revolver from my pocket and threatened to eradicate the culprits, the parents continue to laugh.

The children are dressed to kill. Girls are covered, head to toe, in pink and carry around every stereotypical girlie item you can think of. The boys, hair quiffed and coiffed from the moment the first fine sprouts appear on their scalps, do precisely what they want when they want. Discipline is an alien concept to Italian parents.

It's common to see huge *bambini* with babies' dummies stuck firmly in their mouths and doting dads carrying and cuddling overweight and over-indulged sons who must be ten years old. To an observing Brit, it seems extraordinary and you wonder how these pampered children can possibly grow up to be self-sufficient, well balanced adults, yet somehow they do.

Hypochondria

Tell an Italian that your left ear-lobe aches and you can bet he or she will have a remedy, and usually a bizarre one. Stand on your head, eat a bowl of tortellini drenched in artichoke salsa and chant three Hail Marys - everything will be fine, except on the third Friday in Lent.

It's not only the extraordinary range of old wives' recipes that characterises so many Italians – it is their out-and-out hypochondria. Ask them how they are and they're unlikely to say they're feeling fine, or even that they're a little under the weather: they will say that their liver is not working too well this week or that their appendix is out of sorts. How you feel when one of these important bodily parts is not performing at its best is something I neither know nor particularly want to, but most Italians can trace every under-par symptom to a specific cell or two on their body and concoct the appropriate remedy for it.

Caring, sharing and staring

Ah, the Italians – so friendly, so welcoming, always have a smile on their face. That's the foreigner's image and belief, but is it the reality? Well, no more than it is anywhere else, actually. Are the English friendly? Or the Scots? The Germans? And the answer to all these questions is: some are and some aren't.

In Montottone, we encountered all sorts. There were some people who welcomed us from day one, always greeted us with a smile, were ever eager to help us find our way through the many day-to-day obstacles of Italian life. They would always be happy to talk, even if our limited language skills in our early days made us hard work. They would wave if they spotted us driving past or at the far side of the square.

Emanuela in Bar Rosita always greeted us warmly, smilingly served our 'Café Inglese' as we hilariously called Café Americano, and was never afraid to be drawn into some complex and confused conversation, usually centred on when we arrived, how long we were staying, when we were returning to England, and how was the weather in the UK. Serena, our usual waitress at La Brocca, the family-run village restaurant, always welcomed us back with a hug and a fusillade of high-speed gossip, some of which we almost understood.

It was a similar story of warmth, smiles and helpfulness from others in the village: Giuseppe at the garage; Maurizio at the petrol station, Mara in the village supermarket, Sara in the little grocery shop, Simone and Anna-Maria in another of our favourite restaurants a few miles away. They were all far more than just straightforward friendly, they were enthusiastic, chatty, embracing and ever anxious to help us in any way they could and to make us welcome.

Yet for all that this kindness warmed us, we could never understand how it was that some of Montottone's other residents seemed, if not hostile, then distinctly unfriendly towards us. Even after twelve years, there were several locals who either could not bring themselves to acknowledge when we greeted them with an undemanding 'buongiorno' or who simply stared at us as you might an animal in a zoo, oblivious to their own blatant rudeness. We wrote it off as ignorance; maybe it was just plain old-fashioned stupidity. Perhaps Montottone had more than its share of village idiots, but we and other expat friends experienced the same staring culture in other rural towns and villages in Italy.

The Italian way

The plague of antisocial behaviour, often fuelled by alcohol, has spread across Europe. The Brits are as bad as anyone in that respect and, although the continent's more southerly nations are less badly affected, the problem exists everywhere. In Italy, we hear tales of drunkenness and violent disorder taking place in some of the major cities but in all our years in Le Marche, we never once saw a drunk – not even a British drunk! Few people seemed to drink beer and much of the wine that was consumed tended to be young, local stuff that had the alcoholic kick of a tired hamster. Even at public events where plastic cups of wine were being sold more cheaply than the water, most people had no more than a cup or two of wine and the water was equally popular.

Similarly, we very rarely saw outbursts of real anger, although shows of frustration were common enough, understandably so considering the bureaucratic jungle that so dominates proceedings. Nor did we ever witness a fight. Sometimes Italians appear to be having a furious exchange, with waving arms and loud threats, when, in fact, it is their normal means of communicating; they're actually chatting excitedly about their grandchildren or their lunch.

From our experience, Italians generally dislike confrontation of any kind. Many is the time that we have been driven half-demented by some crass or ludicrous action, but when we have displayed our anger, we have been met with disarming smiles, over-the-top apologies, complicated explanations and, sometimes, a satisfactory outcome.

Like many Europeans living cheek by jowl on the continent, the Italians appear to have no real sense of personal space. They will swarm around you, crowd you, shout to one another even when most of the noise is going straight into your unprepared ear; they simply seem not even to notice your presence. We Brits are an island nation with an insular mentality and we prize our personal space. It's not like that in Italy and it can take some getting used to.

Italy is far from alone in having what might euphemistically be called a cash culture but it takes a little time for Brits to understand properly, if we ever do. A great many services or small businesses will happily give a *sconto* (discount) for a cash transaction that, one presumes, does not need to go through their books and therefore need not arouse the interest of the taxman. Yet so deep-rooted is the fear of the *Guardia di Finanza* – the Finance Police – that many shop or café owners will rush out after you if you should leave the premises without your *scontrino* (receipt).

We came to know many Italians during our years in Le Marche and, if such generalisations have any value at all, we would say that most fell into one of two categories: one group had a bit of money and embraced *la bella figura*, with flash cars, expensive clothing and an abundance of the latest designer kit inside and outside the home; the other category comprised those struggling to make ends meet, who spluttered around in beaten-up old cars and staved off the worst of winter with layers of unflattering clothing rather than expensive central heating – but had shelves groaning under the weight of books and who knew the flora and fauna and Italy's seasons as well as their grandparents had.

The ex-pats we knew also tended to fall into one of two categories: those with considerable wherewithal who had the financial clout to smooth out any problems they might encounter, and those who had to make every euro count. Many of our ex-pat friends fitted comfortably into the former group and, while I would accuse none of them of extravagance or ostentatiousness, their relative wealth did seem to insulate them from many of the everyday irritations that arose. The less well-off, a group in which Rosie and I undoubtedly belonged, spent a disproportionate amount of our time doing battle with something or other. At least one British couple of our acquaintance, lured into buying a rural wreck after watching an episode of 'A Place in the Sun', lived almost like squatters and had to return to England every few months to earn enough cash to pay for the next refurbishment work on Casa Nightmare.

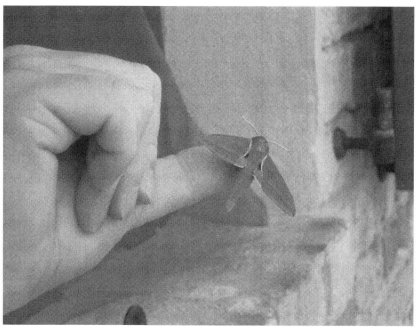

A spectacular moth that dropped in for a visit one night.

Surreal encounters

Every ex-pat who has ever spent a serious amount or time in Italy will certainly have a fund of stories to tell of surreal moments or occasions they have experienced. We had far too many to recall, but I shall attempt to describe a few that have stuck firmly in my mind.

The wedding party 1

Lorella and Oreste, our dear friends from Montottone's *pensione*, invited us to be guests at a wedding party they were hosting for friends. The newlyweds were a local girl, whose parents were friends of Lorella, and her Japanese bridegroom. They had married in the morning at one of the village's five churches, and the wedding lunch was being staged in Lorella's vast kitchen-dining room because the bride's parents' home nearby was far too small.

The assembled guests were, to put it mildly, a mixed bunch. Rosie and I were the only Brits present. The groom, his sister and parents were Japanese. He had met his bride while she was working in Tokyo. He spoke perfect Italian and English. His parents spoke only Japanese. The best man was from Taiwan and spoke fluent Japanese and English but not Italian. The rest of the gathering were Italians, bar one or two young men whose nationality was indiscernible. The Italian bride spoke some Japanese but no English; her parents spoke Montottonese dialect Italian and seemed totally bewildered by everything that was going on around them. We formed the opinion that they had probably never ventured far from Montottone and believed Tokyo was somewhere east of Venice.

We found ourselves seated between the English-speaking Taiwanese best man and the groom's parents who, apparently, had never before left Japan. Conversation with the best man was straightforward and interesting, but with the father of the groom it was just about impossible. He spoke to no-one other than his silent wife, and absolutely no-one spoke with him. I made a couple of unsuccessful attempts, using either sign language or employing words that I thought would have global resonance – like motorcycle names or electronics firms. How I manoeuvred Honda into any sort of conversation, I cannot now imagine.

I remembered that, in the past, when my Italian was still very limited, I had on occasion bonded with Oreste, who spoke no English and dialect Italian, by 'talking' football. Like me he was a football fan and was always ready to exchange gossip and opinions about the events of the day. He would shout 'Inter' at me and put up his thumb; I would respond with a cry of 'Chelsea', and we would show approval for such *calcio* superstars as Zola and Vialli. Oh, how we laughed. I guess you had to be there . . .

So I thought I would employ the same policy with my Japanese co-diner, who seemed preoccupied and slightly horrified by the mountain of pasta that had been plonked down in front of him. 'Nagoya Grampus Eight', I blurted out with a wide grin on my face and a raised thumb to indicate approval. It was the only Japanese football club I had ever heard of because England's own Gary Lineker had played for them at the end of his career. Father of the groom looked at me as though I had just vomited on his plate, before responding with a small, inscrutable smile. Was it acknowledgement of the merits of Nagoya Grampus Eight? Appreciation of my feeble efforts to be friendly when everyone around him was ignoring him? Was it disdain for a dim Englishman obsessed with such a non-cerebral pastime as football? Was it a build-up of wind as a result of the pasta? Who could say?

All around us the chatter was loud and incessant, with even more Italian arm-waving than usual because of the language and cultural barriers. But the groom's parents remained ignored, silent and clearly wishing more than anything else that they were back in Tokyo, speaking Japanese with Japanese friends and eating Japanese food.

Suddenly the room erupted into panic and chaos, something at which the Italians are so practised: someone – perhaps the groom but maybe not – realised that the bride had been missing since the antipasto an hour earlier. Silence was called for and we could just make out the plaintive calls of the bride from upstairs. She had got stuck in the bathroom. The lock had jammed. First Oreste had to be scolded because he had failed to get the lock fixed, despite repeated instructions from Lorella. Then some of the diners put down their forks and set off upstairs to rescue the girl. Lorella's father Mario led the charge. A few minutes later, the blushing bride was back at the table and being force-fed the pasta course that she had almost missed. There was much sympathy and wringing of hands. Rosie and I were the only people who found the whole episode hilarious. We put on our serious faces, though.

Ivo's car travails

Another graphic example of Italian sense of humour failure came with the sort of slapstick moment that is an everyday occurrence in Italy.

At Casa Rosa, we had a number of concrete posts that had, for many years, been used to support the wire on which our grape vines grew. When some of the vines were removed by the *contadini* so that we had some space between the end of the vineyard and our terrace, the posts became redundant.

They were maybe ten or so feet in length, solid concrete and wickedly heavy. I could manage to lift one end at a time and swing them around, so moving them out of the way was becoming a time-consuming and exhausting process. Then our neighbour Ivo, Cristina's husband, a street-wise character never slow to take possession of anything that might be of use in the future, offered to help.

He would load them into the back of his battered old Volkswagen Golf and take them away to his storage area - actually an accumulation of junk dumped around a tree on a bit of his land a hundred metres distant. The fact that the posts were far too long to go into the back of his little hatchback and far too heavy to get in there anyway did not deter him in the least; Ivo would never be told anything.

Soon enough, he realised that plan A was not going to work, but he was confident that plan B would. That involved looping a length of heavy wire through the hole at the top of the post and tying it to the back of his car, so the posts could be dragged along the short distance to his stockpile.

He got the first post successfully tied to the rear of the spluttering Golf, which, due to the massive weight at the back, had its front end pointing laughably skywards. But there wasn't far to go. With a massive surge of engine revs from the front and accompanying cloud of smoke from the rear, Ivo began to pull away . . . until a massive bang from the rear halted him after a few feet.

The post lay heavily and defiantly on the ground and attached to it was the entire hatch of Ivo's hatchback, ripped clean off and never properly to be replaced (although we did catch a glimpse of it a few weeks later with the hatch being held in place by a massive web of heavy-duty sticky tape).

Ivo, hands on hips and Italian swear words cascading from his mouth, stood staring aghast first down at the post and hatch on the ground, and then at the gaping hole in the back of his car. Not for the first time, Rosie and I forced ourselves to choke back the laughter because Ivo hardly looked in the mood for fun. He untied the hatch from the now-abandoned post, flung the hatch into the gaping rear of his car and, still mumbling furiously, drove home.

It must have been a traumatic event for Ivo because he had always had a close relationship with his cars. In the days before he and Cristina installed heating in their house, he could often be seen, on bright, cold days, fast asleep in his car. He would move it now and then to ensure he captured and magnified the weak rays of the sun. Cristina kept warm by working quietly in the garden.

The wedding party 2

The Italians are big on BMDs. There are few events better guaranteed to generate over-the-top excitement than a baby, a wedding or a funeral.

One wedding to which we had the privilege of being invited was truly unforgettable; to call it lavish would be to seriously undersell it. The happy couple – I shall not name them out of courtesy – had three teenaged children between them from previous marriages, and had lived together as man and wife for many years. None of that, however, in any way inhibited their plans for a wedding that would impress their friends and neighbours and live long in the memory.

They had booked a huge country house hotel and invited well over one hundred guests. The place was decorated inside and out to within an inch of its life, with bunting and lights, and there was enough food of the highest quality to have fed half of Italy. The drink flowed (though no-one seemed in any way inebriated), the live band played throughout the evening and the dancing went on into the early hours. The bride had been having dance lessons for some time, mainly to ensure her figure was just right for the night, so her ever-indulgent groom had even hired a professional dancer to keep his bride on her toes when his own stamina levels dipped.

The night ended with a firework display; the newlyweds set off on the first of two luxury cruises a few days later. We were invited but had to decline due to other commitments. Then they came back to their village home, their lives returned to what passed for normality, and a couple of years later they divorced.

Unexpected visitors

The bells sounded more of a clank than a tinkle and were barely discernible at first. As they grew louder, we walked out of the house and scanned the surrounding fields for an explanation. In the distance we could make out a presence, but what was it? A vast greyish-white shape of considerable size and it seemed to be moving. As the shape came closer across the hills and valleys towards Casa Rosa, we could see that it was a massive flock of sheep. They had bells hung around their necks and were being guided by a shepherd.

Road block: motorists have to wait when a shepherd is moving his flock.

Eventually the shepherd and his charges appeared on the perimeter of our garden and we walked over to speak to him. His name was Giuliano, he came from a village a few miles away and he explained that it was his routine from time to time to march his flock across the countryside to feed and, at the same time, to keep the grass trimmed. Would we mind if he fenced off an area of our land so that his sheep could graze and our few cultivated plants close to the house would be protected from both sheep teeth and sheep deposits?

We watched, fascinated, as the flock munched their way along the steepest part of our land, before Giuliano, with a melody of whistles and shouts, shepherded them on their way to the next destination.

We had English friends in Giuliano's home village who were looking for someone to mind their house for them while they were back in the UK. As luck would have it, Giuliano's wife was available, always on the lookout for little jobs to help make ends meet, so we put them in touch with one another and everyone, especially the sheep, ended up happy. To this day, Giuliano's wife is still looking after the house for our English friends.

A somewhat less sociable visit occurred at eight o'clock one morning, waking us from our sleep (our nights were usually later when we were in Italy, as were our mornings). The piercing and incessant barking of three dogs and two rough-looking men were scouring our woodland, vineyard and olive fields in search of truffles. Whether or not they were successful, we did not discover but they had gone by the time we had emerged from our morning ablutions.

Moments to cherish

Dotted among the countless highs and lows of our Italian years were many moments or events that we greatly appreciated at the time and would hug to ourselves later. Here are a few examples:

- A visit to the beautiful old theatre in Fermo for an evening of Gershwin, illuminated by a bravura piano performance by a young female music student from Poland. The setting, the atmosphere and the music combined to make a perfect evening.
- Another unforgettable musical experience, this time when we were invited along to the *Conservatorio* at Fermo to attend the graduation ceremony of a young singer friend of ours called Lucia. It was a scorching hot summer afternoon, all the windows of the

magnificent chamber were open and the noise of traffic was a constant distraction. But when Lucia began to sing, her wonderful soprano voice cut through all the background noise and sent goose bumps down the spines of the audience. She graduated with flying colours and has gone on to become a successful professional singer.

- Italians tend to take their extraordinarily rich history for granted, perhaps because they have so much of it, but we never cease to be struck by it all. One afternoon we visited two ancient sites only a few miles from us: the remains of a Roman theatre at Falerone and the Roman Hellenic excavations at Monterinaldo. We had them completely to ourselves - there was no-one else at either of them.

- A hugely enjoyable evening at a watermelon (*cocomero*) festival in Montottone, after which, with friends, we headed into Fermo for the annual *Notte Bianca*, or 'White Night', when the city centre is illuminated all night. Trade and craft stalls line the streets and the vast Piazza di Popolo, and thousands of people of all ages turn out to shop, eat, drink, chat and generally mill about. It seemed odd to us to see very old, often frail people and new-born babies out and about at two in the morning, but the atmosphere, as always, was friendly, sober and relentlessly cheerful. I don't remember us buying anything, but it was a lovely occasion infused with the powerful community spirit of provincial Le Marche.

- Visits to the Sibillini National Park were always wonderfully uplifting – offering a draft of cool, fresh air when the temperatures down below were stifling and catch-your-breath views at any time of year. Sometimes the drive high up into the mountains could be a little disconcerting, especially when meeting another vehicle coming the other way on the narrow tracks. Once we pulled over to allow a car to come past and the driver stopped, lowered his window and greeted us warmly; it was Gianni, a builder who had done some work for us a few months earlier. I well remember one visit to the *Campolungo* at the Amandola Refuge on a beautiful spring day. We enjoyed a delicious, leisurely picnic, walked among the beautiful flora and admired the incredible views from high on Monte Sibilla. Best of all, we did not see another person in all the time we were up there.

The unadulterated beauty of the Sibillini National Park is always captivating.

- We also loved the marvellous feeling of having a special place all to ourselves on many of the occasions when we went to the beach to swim. Conscious of lacking the requisite *bella figura*, as well as being distinctly under-bronzed, we tended to go for a swim in the warm Adriatic at dusk when most of the beautiful bodies had sashayed off home. The pebbled beach at Altidona was our favourite spot, not because we preferred its stones to the glorious sand at other beaches but because it was easily accessible and comparatively under-populated. *(See 'We dip our toes into Italian beach life' below).*

Our favourite beach at Altidona.

One unforgettable evening in July 2010, we booked the entire terrace area of La Brocca, the village restaurant, for a celebration of Rosie's birthday. We invited a total of twenty guests of various nationalities: British and Italians, of course, plus Canadians, a German and a couple of New Zealanders. Two of our friends played guitar and sang, and a delightful singer from the village added her voice, too. It was a hot, sultry evening but the air was thick with the scent of jasmine, the food was terrific and the memories remain vivid and cheering.

- Over the years we became firm friends with the *contadini* family who farmed our land. They looked after our vines, olives and fields and in return paid us rent in the form of jugs of wine, olive oil and occasional vegetables. It was a good arrangement: every extra yard of land they could cultivate meant a little more income for the family, while we never had to concern ourselves with caring for any of the crops. The first time they knocked on our door to hand us the rent, we were delighted to see that the red and white wine and the olive oil had been augmented by a bag full of tomatoes from their *orto* and a cooked chicken, which turned out to be tough and stringy; it had also been neatly packaged with its head tucked tidily up its own bottom.

Our 'rent' from the contadini, with wine, oil tomatoes and melons as the currency.

- Once, when the *contadini* were hoping we would renew the rental agreement (which we did), they invited us to lunch with the family. They were all in attendance for their daily ritual: Filippo, the head of the family; his tiny smiley wife Rosa, whose life was devoted to feeding the family; sons Valeriano and Luigi and their wives. It was a lovely happy occasion and, if the conversation did not exactly flow, there was enough mutual understanding to make it enjoyable. The women showed us the small cubicles they had created in a hangar-like building behind the house where they were employed doing piecework for a local shoe manufacturer. It put a different spin on the term 'working from home', especially when we learnt that they worked there all through the year, with no heating. They were paid a pitifully low rate for their work, even though we noted that some of the sports shoes they had completed bore designer names.

- Our frequent long absences from Casa Rosa made it difficult to cultivate much because drought or rampant wildlife would quickly send most plants to their death. We managed lavender, rosemary and other drought-tolerant plants, as well as agave and cactus, which thrived, but planting anything less macho was pointless. However, we had inherited two or three small wild peach trees. Most years our harvest was poor – we suspected, with good reason, that most of their produce was probably going down other throats while we were away. One summer, though, we were in residence for a long period which included the peach harvest. We could hardly believe how many fruits each of the little trees produced. They were small but delicious and featured at breakfast for many days; we gave away basketfuls and many more remained inaccessible on the trees.

A small part of our harvest from one of our wild peach trees.

- Only once during our years of owning Casa Rosa did
  we spend the Christmas and New Year period there,
  and it was magical. On Christmas Eve we were invited
  to Lorella's home to eat with the family. Her mother
  Ines had conjured up some interesting and delicious
  antipasti dishes, and Mario had made classic
  Marchigiani *brodetto*, with thirteen different types of
  fish. It was a wonderfully happy evening. It was
  surprising, if not embarrassing, that we succeeded in
  having Christmas lunch the next day at La Brocca, the
  Montottone restaurant. It comprised no fewer than
  sixteen stomach-stretching courses, of which a few
  thankfully were liquid. La Brocca was beautifully
  bedecked for the occasion and packed with happy,
  chattering diners. New Year was welcomed in at a
  party in a sprawling six-storey house in the nearby
  little town of Petritoli. It was owned by an Englishman
  and his American wife, whom we knew mainly

through our neighbours Ivo and Cristina. The Italian guests present were great company, including an odd character, who went by the name of Dennis and was dressed all in black, including a hat and shades. At midnight we were impressed to see, from our high vantage point, the whole area illuminated by fireworks shooting into the sky from hilltop villages for miles around. Another highlight of that mid-winter visit, with its lovely, clear spring-like weather, came on our wedding anniversary, January 4, when we visited the historic city of Macerata, one of Le Marche's regional capitals but not one that we knew well. We strolled along the city's handsome buildings and beautiful squares, located its famous amphitheatre (closed, of course) and gazed in wonderment at the many shop windows displaying grotesque models of the *Befana*, the witch, whose festival day is January 6.

- Maybe not exactly a moment to cherish but pleasing and worth reporting nonetheless. More than once we turned a corner on one of the roads out of Montottone to encounter a police car at the roadside and a smartly uniformed officer striding out to stop us for a routine vehicle check (in rural Le Marche, there is not too much else to keep the police occupied, as a Carabinieri friend of ours once confided). But as soon as he clapped eyes on our right-hand drive car with its UK number plates, he stepped swiftly out of the way and anxiously waved us past. We knew it was because dealing with the untold complexities of checking a foreign vehicle – and in all probability having to deal with a foreign driver who spoke no Italian – was far too much trouble. It happened to us a number of times. Although our car was always legal, Rosie and I had agreed that, were we to be stopped by police for a possible speeding infringement, we would stick resolutely to English and pretend to understand not a word they were saying.

- The steep track down to our house was a recurring problem for us though all our years of ownership. It was slippery and treacherous in icy weather, bone hard and badly rutted in periods of drought, but never worse than during periods of incessant rain that could often last for weeks. Then it turned into a quagmire; the mud could be deep and horribly sticky, especially on the parts of the road that were overhung with trees so that the drying wind could not do its work. We encountered this scenario fairly early in our ownership of Casa Rosa when we were still using rental cars, invariably lightweight little jobs with the ruggedness of a roller-skate. Returning to the house in heavy rain after a trip into the village, we turned into our road and were immediately aware of a sharp deterioration in the surface. Even at walking pace, the car wanted to turn sideways and when we had slithered up the slight incline to the area near the trees, the mud took control of the car and carried it sideways into the deepest of the mire. We managed to extricate ourselves but the car was obviously not going anywhere; the mud was above the top of its wheels. We could have abandoned it and sploshed our way down the track to the house a few hundred yards away, laden with groceries we had just bought. But would we ever be able to ascend the slope again on foot to retrieve the stricken car? We did what we so often did when we met trouble in Italy – we phoned Lorella. Lorella phoned her father Mario, and within a few minutes he arrived in his muscular Toyota 4x4 with the intention of hauling our car out of its mess. It did not take him more than a few seconds to realise that exercise would have quickly resulted in his 4x4 meeting the same fate, so he turned around and returned minutes later at the wheel of his tractor. (We never really knew why Mario owned a tractor but it was his pride and joy). It powered through the cloying mud with ease, dragged our miserable little hire car free and our latest stressful adventure ended happily. From that day on, we called him Super Mario – Mario Salvatore, our hero of the hour.

Rosie wrote this in 2012 about our relationship with the Adriatic beaches:

We dip our toes into Italian beach life

Here in the full glare of Italy's summer, holiday time means only one thing to the Italians – bronzy bronzy on the beachy beachy. From morning until early evening they lie out on their colour-coded sunbeds like so many identical offcuts of gleaming mahogany, occasionally reaching out for a drink that's been delivered to their personal side-table.

For them, the sea has two functions: for reflecting the sun's glare on to them, and, when life on the rotisserie has become just too tedious, for mincing along its edge where the water is just deep enough to make beautiful iridescent patterns around their dainty ankles. This being Italy, that activity applies to the men as well as to the women. Beach life here is Very Important. Being seen on the right beach in the right get-up counts for a lot. There are Them and Us areas, with public and private sections strictly marked out and six-pack sentries on duty to eject riff-raff who dare set foot on the wrong side.

Naturally, for a pair of English ragamuffins like me and David, it all seems a very long way from the full-on rigours of the Dorset coast. However, we're keen to take some exercise, if only to prove to ourselves that day after day of eating, drinking, sleeping and reading (and habitually falling asleep while so doing) has not depleted our muscle tone to danger levels. Personally, I'm concerned that just moving out of a chair will propel my heart rate into the upper hundreds.

So we head to the beach with the idea of taking a swim. Obviously, knowing what we know, we time our arrival for after everyone has gone home, lest the lily-white hue of our skin should dazzle and shock. It does seem silly that even though we don't know anyone here, I still wouldn't want to be 'seen'. There's always the concern that one day, minding my own business around the cereals aisle of a drab supermarket back home, some exotic Italian might exclaim: "Hey, Mario, ees ze donna bianca! Zee marble-white lady we laughed at on the beach, you remember?"

Only a few slabs of mahogany remain on our chosen (public, free) beach, drawing the last of the sun's rays as the tide ebbs. David and I set up our camp – folding chairs, a couple of towels, a bottle of water, and then we change and tiptoe and wince our way across the pebbles and over the sand into the turquoise water. It's so warm it is almost more of a shock to the system than if it were ice-cold, which is what we're used to.

I bounce about from foot to foot, convincing myself that this isn't typical territory for sharks, and wondering what to do next. When you're used to thrashing up and down the lane of an indoor pool it isn't easy knowing how to recreate that same feeling of superwoman achievement in the unconfined expanse of the Adriatic Sea.

Squinting into the setting sun, I swim as fast as I can towards a promontory. After several minutes I stop to assess my progress. I seem to have moved about a yard closer to the landmark and about four-and-a-half inches away from David. What's happening? I panic that I have slipped into a terrifying dimension in which things are not what they seem.

Then I remember I'm in Italy, where nothing is ever as you expect it to be. I relax, splash about a bit, and later on I have some more wine. It is, I feel, necessary to celebrate our initiation into Italian beach life, albeit in unique Dorset style.

Moments to remember

Some of the more memorable events of our Italian years have lodged in our memories for less happy reasons.

We were woken in the middle of the night on April 6, 2009, by tremors that hardly registered with us at the time – but the next morning we discovered that there had been a massive earthquake at L'Aquila in the Abruzzo region to the south of us. Around three hundred people had died that night, including at least twenty children. Another 1,500 residents of the great city were injured. As many as eleven thousand buildings were damaged, many reduced to rubble, and around sixty-five thousand – the great majority of the old city's inhabitants – were left homeless.

We had Italian friends in Abruzzo who, we knew, had relatives in L'Aquila. When we phoned to check, we learned that they had survived but their home had been destroyed. Italy was in shock and even in our neighbouring region, Le Marche, there was a strong sense of despair and sadness. Earthquakes are something the people of central Italy, near the Apennine Mountain chain, have had to learn to live with, and die with, over the centuries, but it is something nobody ever fully comes to terms with. A few days after the main quake, Casa Rosa shook again in one of the numerous aftershocks. We knew at once what it was and felt heavy hearts realising that our minor tremor probably meant that more homes had been destroyed less than forty miles to the south.

Rosie wrote this piece at the time:

Tremors of an earthquake leave us all shaken

A quite extraordinary thing has happened this week, and I am incredibly lucky and grateful to be here to record it.
David and I have slunk off for a quiet Easter break at our house in Italy but within a couple of days of arriving here, we found ourselves in the outer ripples of il terremoto, the catastrophic earthquake that hit L'Aquila in the early hours of Monday.

Its great rumble woke us, shaking not just the bed but the whole bedroom. I haven't felt so frightened or so helpless since a lightning bolt hit a plane in which I was an already nervous passenger (that was over Italy, too, but let's put it down to coincidence).

The shaking of il terremoto lasted about half a minute but even before it had emitted its final deathly roll I heard alarmed dogs start to bark – a sure sign, at that pre-dawn hour, that they'd been alerted by some act of God, not man.

As I set about restoring my heart to its proper place I noted the time, 3.33am, and saw David had returned to Nod, from which he had only briefly been disturbed. That left me to try and work it all out: it must have been an earthquake, of that I was sure, but I had no way of knowing how bad it had been. It had felt frightening, but having never experienced an earthquake before I had nothing to compare it with. So I took the line of least resistance, blanked it all out and went back to sleep.

In the morning everything started to become clear, as we listened to the reports on the radio and translated some of the less hysterical stuff. A woman living nearby came to tell us that she'd been aware of several tremors over the past week so hadn't been surprised by the strength of the 'quake, even though it was 35 miles away as the crow flies.

We once passed through L'Aquila, the city that sits on a mountain-top perch, when driving to Pompeii. We should have stopped then, but didn't, chasing the clock and wanting to put kilometres behind us. Now we'll never know how spectacular its 13th century church of Santa Maria di Collemaggio might have looked, its perfect rose window set into a pink and white marble façade: we hear that it has been terribly damaged.

But of course it's the people that are rightly the focus of everyone's thoughts and concerns. With a rising death toll of unimaginable proportions and countless thousands badly hurt and homeless, it is a tragedy and a human crisis almost beyond comprehension in a European country of the modern age.

Mid-afternoon on Monday I took a deep breath and called an Italian friend whose husband, Peppe, comes from L'Aquila. They themselves live 20 miles east of the city, nearer the coast. "What news of the family?" I asked, helplessly.

She said that Peppe had been sitting for hours hunched in front of the TV, looking like a ghost and unable to believe what he was watching. Mamma, who lives with them, had been wearing her coat since dawn, ready to make a dash for it. "I am too young to die!" she kept exclaiming, ignoring the fact that her 92-year-old legs can scarcely carry her downstairs, let alone away to safety.

Novelia told me: "Peppe has three brothers and a sister in L'Aquila and they have all lost their homes, beautiful houses in the old centre of the city, and all their belongings. They have nothing left but their lives, but they know they are the lucky ones."

There is little one can say in response to that – in any language.

This was Rosie's follow-up article a week later:

Not so much a picnic as a feat of stamina

We are still in Italy, happily – or so we confidently hope – post-earthquake. There were several after-shocks following the terrible 'terremoto' that so devastated L'Aquila and its outlying villages at the beginning of last week. The most recent one that we felt was last Thursday when, at about 9.40pm, I heard a great cracking, rolling sound, like a long thunderclap. I was just exclaiming to David, "Did you hear that?" when the house and everything in it shook violently. Instinctively, I clung on to the dining-table, where I was sitting. It was only later that I realised I would have been better off throwing myself under it, but, just like witty ripostes, you always thinking of the clever follow-through when it's too late.

The tremor was just a tiddler, 4.4 at its core in the Abruzzo region, to the south of us in Le Marche, compared with the deadly 6.9 of a few days before. Nevertheless, I still felt as though everything was still dancing around under me long after the shaking stopped.

That's enough of earthquakes and after-shocks for me for a lifetime, I've decided. Even when the epicentre is a long way away and we really aren't in any danger, they are very unnerving.

Fortunately, there has been the delightful distraction of Easter to focus upon, and of course in Italy this is an event that quite eclipses the UK equivalent, which amounts to a few days off work for stuffing ourselves silly with chocolate.

The Italians, as you might expect, really go to town with their celebrations, since Easter is not only at the heart of their religious beliefs but also marks the end of winter's gloom and the start of spring's dazzling, sunny days.

There is a proverb in Italy – natale con i tuoi, pasqua con chi vuoi – which translates as 'Christmas with your own (as in family and relatives), Easter with whom you wish'. This means that it is a great time for friends to come together and make merry, which they frequently do by taking picnics out into the countryside.

For those less inclined to pack up a pizza and trundle off to sit in a sunbeam among the poppies, restaurants like the one here in the village put on a feast that runs to about eight courses. Not so much a picnic, then, as a feat of stamina.

In the interests of cultural research, we booked in at La Brocca, teaming up with an Italian, a Canadian, two New Zealanders, a German and a rock musician from Sheffield to fill a table of decidedly cosmopolitan origins.

I am delighted to report that Dorset held its own manfully, and David and I did not disappoint in the plate-clearing stakes (veterans' category).

Interestingly, such is the Italians' passion to please that they prepared several separate dishes for me, the one diner among 200 who was a non-meat eater. I said when we booked that I would be happy either to sit out a particular course or just nibble on vegetables, but they dismissed such madness and insisted my feast should be just as grand and enjoyable as everyone else's.

The lunch, which lasted a mere six hours, was a joy and delight, with not a single person worse the wear for drink, not one child misbehaving and nothing but good-natured happiness prevailing. Only one thing troubled me slightly in all that time: a couple, presumably Italian, sitting at a table close to ours in total silence throughout. They looked so miserable and disenchanted, lost in their unhappy thoughts, that I couldn't help thinking how much better off they'd have been if they'd followed the advice of the proverb and celebrated Easter with friends. Anything, anywhere, rather than 'with their own', the poor things.

Four years on, almost to the day, Rosie and I drove to L'Aquila to see it for ourselves and monitor progress on the rebuilding. This is the article I wrote in April 2013:

L'Aquila's nightmare four years on

Four years on from the earthquake that shattered the medieval city of L'Aquila, a pall of sadness still hangs over the historic centre. Most of the narrow, cobbled streets in the heart of Abruzzo's capital are still out of bounds, a 'zona rossa' cordoned off behind metal fences while the gigantic task of restoration inches forward.

In the streets immediately around L'Aquila's closed heart, all is eerily quiet. There are a few people, mostly involved in the rebuilding work, and one or two small shops and cafes have been reopened by owners driven by courage or desperation. But customers are few, tourists are non-existent, houses and entire streets are boarded-up, deserted, abandoned.

This once-proud city has the appearance and poignancy of a war zone and offers few indications that former glories will ever be recaptured. The quake that tore it apart in April 2009 smashed more than the city's fabric; it seems to have broken its spirit.

The mountain city of L'Aquila was at the epicentre of the earthquake with a magnitude of 6.3, the deadliest to hit Italy in almost 30 years. Even now accurate figures are still vague by but the death toll was around 300 people, including at least 20 children. Another 1,500 residents were injured. As many as 11,000 buildings were damaged, many reduced to rubble, and around 65,000 people – the great majority of the old city's inhabitants – were left homeless.

The impact of the quake was felt right across the huge central Italian region of Abruzzo, as far away as Rome and in the neighbouring regions of Lazio, Le Marche, Molise, Umbria and Campania.

There have been many thousands of aftershocks, and at least 30 of them had a Richter Scale magnitude of more than 3.5. L'Aquila continues to hold its breath.

I had been in Italy, some 40 miles north in Le Marche, when I was woken by the vibration in the early hours of April 6, 2009.

The next morning we learnt of the cause and of the ferocity of the quake, and spoke by phone to friends whose relatives had seen their property destroyed. But only now, four years on, did I witness close-up the consequences of the force of nature that had disturbed my sleep.

Wandering around the accessible areas of L'Aquila's broken centre felt at times like an intrusion on a family's private grief. So many once-handsome buildings boarded up, propped up with massive steel or timber girders, and it was easy to see how very lovely it must have been and hard to imagine that it could ever be again.

The barista in the little café greeted her few customers with a smile but admitted her sadness at the devastation all around. The proprietor of one of the very few shops actually operating seemed pleased to glimpse even a passer-by – a customer would have been too much to expect.

Cranes tower over the fragile, precarious buildings as workmen pick their way through trying to bring order and hope to the scene and they chatter and laugh as building site workmen do the world over. But through the eyes of a visitor, it seems as though they are merely going through the motions to keep alive the dreams of the city's displaced, heartbroken people. L'Aquila is Italian for eagle. On my visit, the air felt heavy with pessimism. It is hard to imagine the eagle soaring again.

Another unpleasant memory of our time in Italy was on a far more personal scale and it showed us the kind, considerate side that we have seen so often in Italians, especially in difficult circumstances.

On our day of departure for England, Rosie was taken ill with what turned out to be a painful bladder infection. She was sick at Ancona airport and there was a real danger that she may be refused permission to fly. The airport staff, however, were brilliant and compassionate, as was a young doctor called to help, and eventually we were able to board the plane, albeit as the last passengers.

The end in sight

Insomuch as we had ever actually planned anything properly with regard to our Italian adventure, we had always expected that we would have Casa Rosa for maybe ten years. We would then sell it – for a healthy profit, of course – and use the lump sum to supplement our pension pot which had been slimmed down by our decision to leave our jobs ahead of time.

What we and thousands of other ex-pats in Italy, France, Spain and elsewhere, had failed to factor in to our plans was a massive world-wide economic recession, which had made Casa Rosa worth far less than it might have been and removed a vast number of potential buyers from the equation.

The house was on the market for over two years and for the greater part of that time, we were perfectly happy to carry on owning and enjoying the place. There were even times when we considered removing the house from the market because we were so relishing the Italian dimension of our lives.

But in 2013, after a couple of truly glorious visits to Italy, the many down sides, tiresomely listed previously, conspired to convince us that we needed to get out. During a two-week visit in September and October of that year, Italy threw everything at us and left us desperate to get back to England and despairing at the prospect of another year – or more! – having to cope with the burden.

On this visit, a pincer attack from determined wildlife and super-flaky technology almost brought us to our knees. The first setback was the unexpected refusal of our car to start when we arrived from England; the flat battery problem was soon overcome but it set the tone.

Then we discovered that our Italian cellphone had, somehow, been enrolled in a 'plan' whereby the phone company TIM had been taking two euros a week from its balance, meaning we had no credit and could make no calls. So impenetrable are TIM's various tariffs and schemes that we don't know to this day how or why it happened but it took several visits to their shops and at least one angry outburst to solve the issue. The biggest technological nuisance was the appalling service of GetBy, our broadband so-called providers. The link was not working on our arrival – a Saturday – so we had no internet until the Monday. And then the connection was off as often as it was on for the duration of our visit. It was the ninth time we had booked the service in advance of our arrival, and the eighth time it had not been working. They never knew why, they never apologised and they never overcame the problem. When you need internet and email to earn your living, its unreliability is crippling.

Fiamma, our gas suppliers, contacted us to demand payment because our Banca Marche, the world's worst bank, had, for absolutely no logical reason, suddenly decided to stop processing our direct debit.

On the wildlife front, we had to deal with the constant bombardment from the thousands of hornets that had taken possession of our shed and made the south side of the house out of bounds; we were constantly being bitten by spiteful *pappataci* every time we ventured outside - and all too frequently inside the house too; and a plague of moles (or maybe just one busy one) had returned to transform the back grass into something resembling the Sibillini foothills.

The whole gloomy scenario was further compounded by our own dodgy health: Rosie had badly sprained her ankle a month earlier and it was showing no signs of improving and the pain was as bad as ever; I had caught a horrible but short-lived cold and was now inexplicably troubled by a stiff neck.

Despite glorious weather, we were both struggling with our morale by the midway stage of the visit. We had experienced all these problems before, of course, but never quite to this extent and never all at once. It seemed like an omen, a sign that our time was up. So complete was our discontentment that we implemented an impromptu change of plan: we left Casa Rosa three days early and drove back to the UK, forgoing our flight tickets. We closed the house for the winter and cancelled plans to visit again at the end of October.

Farewell, Casa Rosa

In November 2013, exactly a month after arriving back in England having driven our car back from Italy, we set off in the opposite direction – this time in a hired one-ton Volkswagen Transporter van. We had sold Casa Rosa. It had come unexpectedly and quickly but, because of our busy schedule until the New Year – and because the Dutch buyers wanted completion before Christmas – we had to remove our belongings and tie up many loose ends in Italy.
We set off from Dorset in a near-empty van and arrived back home nine days and 2,375 miles later, the van packed with personal effects and a few items of furniture and all the business successfully achieved.
Although the date for the *rogito* – the completion of the sale, to be held at the *notaio*'s office in the nearby town of Civitanova Marche – was not until December 13, that would be dealt with by our agent acting as our proxy so this visit effectively marked the end of our twelve-year romance with Le Marche. We felt a mix of emotions but predominantly relief: the time had come to move on.

After spending our last-ever night in Casa Rosa, we were up early to take our recycling to the depot in a nearby village. Then, after breakfast in a café, it was back to the house for several hours of purposeful mayhem. Various friends and acquaintances arrived to help themselves to our now-unrequired belongings. Later, alone at the little house, we loaded the van with the few things for which we had room and gave Casa Rosa a final, thorough clean.

We were in a swirl of different emotions as we looked around the house that we had grown to know so well, to love so much and, sometimes, to resent. We struggled not to weep but, as the warm, sunny day suddenly clouded over and the rain began to fall, we set off up the track for the last time; our feelings were mainly elation and relief.

We stayed that night with friends and next morning, in a howling gale and lashing rain, we set off in the van for Civitanova Marche, where we were to meet our agent and go to the *notaio*'s office to finalise the proxy arrangements. We waited more than an hour for the *notaio* to be free, despite the long-arranged appointment - presumably he had coffee to finish or needed an urgent snooze. But the technicalities were completed surprisingly quickly. We lobbed out vast sums of cash to the *notaio*, the agent and a few passers-by, went for lunch and then pointed the van north and hit the road bound for England.

The weather had grown worse and the storm was raging as we headed up the A14 *autostrada*. Driving conditions were as bad as we had ever experienced in Italy and we were stunned to see a petrol tanker upside down and engulfed in flames on the opposite carriageway. It was as though Italy was agreeing that it was time for us to go back to England.

Homeward-bound: the rental van is packed with our belongings as we head home to England.

Dolce

An eminent Italian once wrote that Italy is a wonderful place to visit and an awful place to live. I'm not sure I would altogether agree with the second part of the sentence but I can certainly understand and sympathise with the sentiment.

The longer that Rosie and I owned our little piece of Italy, while the topsy-turvy journey took us through countless highs and lows, the overall trajectory was undoubtedly downwards. Our love for the country endured and will probably always do so, but it had become tarnished by events.

For a good year after our escape from Le Marche in the teeth of that ferocious Adriatic coastal storm, our memories of those years in Italy were dominated by the many negatives that befell us towards the end: the bureaucracy that makes reasonable people want to scream in frustration or commit murder; the incompetence and full-on rudeness of some major businesses; the unending bombardment that nature can inflict in the form of hornets, biting flies, hungry wild boar and triffid-like invasive grass; and so much more.

But once the wounds had lost their awful rawness and we were able again to look back through a more accurate and balanced prism, we remembered more vividly some of Italy's glories: the climate (usually); the food and the Italians' understandable pride in it; the heart-melting charm of so many Italians; the indescribable beauty of the landscape, with its mountains and coastline; the achingly beautiful medieval churches and other buildings everywhere from the biggest cities to the smallest villages.

We knew that, from now on, our relationship with Italy would be confined to holidays and in 2014 that yearning for a taste of *Il Bel Paese* led to a wonderful trip to Sicily's gritty capital Palermo and the small Tuscan gem that is Lucca. The holidays confirmed what we had hoped: that Italy, without the burden of home ownership, really is a joyous country.

We began 2015 with another holiday in Sicily, this time staying in ancient Syracuse, and then in April we returned to spend a week in Le Marche for the first time since selling Casa Rosa eighteen months earlier. We rented an apartment in Porto San Giorgio, the small coastal town we knew well, and enjoyed a beautiful, relaxing week, blessed throughout by glorious weather.

On one day we drove to our old village, Montottone, to have coffee in Bar Rosita, lunch in La Brocca, and walk around the *centro storico* once again, relishing the memories and noting just how little had changed in eighteen months. We drove, too, to the little road running parallel to ours and stared across the valley to see Casa Rosa. Its shutters were closed so its new owners were clearly not in residence, but it had gained a smart swimming pool since our day. We felt a twinge of nostalgia, naturally, but the little house had latterly treated us so unkindly that our overriding emotion was one of relief at having disposed of it and we headed back to our rental apartment in carefree mood.

In what was, in effect, our first true holiday in the region, we looked up old friends, and saw Le Marche through very different eyes. It was good company, great food, wonderful countryside, long walks along the near-deserted sandy beach and it all added up to the best real holiday we had ever had. Italy, minus the brain-numbing red tape, was truly paradise. But, of course, it wouldn't be Italy without an injection of nonsense and a dream week had a stressful, frustrating end. The journey from our apartment in Porto San Giorgio began at eight in the morning and finished at our own home almost sixteen hours later.

We got away quickly and easily on another lovely sunny morning, drove to Ancona airport, returned the hire car and checked in our luggage after only a very brief queue. We then had an unexplained four-hour wait before being 'informed' that the fog around the airport meant that no planes would be landing or taking off from there today. It was, to our eyes, slightly hazy but Ancona has a record of being out of action for even the lightest fog.

After an interminable wait, a fleet of three buses arrived to transport all the passengers to Pescara, two hours to the south along the route that we had just driven. The journey defied description: the geriatric driver seemed to be suffering from Parkinson's, so severely was he shaking, and the coach was in a really poor state: a smashed wing mirror, taped-up seats and a gear change that needed both the driver's hands and all his muscle power to achieve. We finally boarded the Ryanair plane six hours after the scheduled departure time.

In May 2016 we spent another week at the same apartment in Porto San Giorgio and enjoyed the visit every bit as much as a year earlier. This is where we want to be, we agreed – but only for holidays. We'll take what we want of the many good bits and the home owners can deal with the rest.

Our visit happily coincided with the classic car race, the *Mille Miglia*, passing through our part of Le Marche. We had long nursed an ambition to have a close-up view of the event so we stationed ourselves among the roadside crowds on the SS16 Adriatic highway as the second leg of the four-day, 1,000-mile odyssey roared through, giving us an unforgettable few hours as we cheered them on their way south. The great event had started the previous day in the northern city of Brescia and was due to finish there after its circuitous route via Rome.

Rosie wrote this about it at the time in 2016:

We witness Carlo's finest hour

We had no idea, when we booked a week's holiday in Italy, that it would coincide with the classic car race, the Mille Miglia, passing close by us. As David and I are both of a petrolhead persuasion, this was a thrill we had no intention of missing: hundreds of the world's most astonishingly beautiful old cars roaring their way along stage 2 of a 1,000-mile circuit from Brescia to Rome and back.

Friends invited us to join them on their balcony to watch the cars as they roared past below. No thanks, we said, we want to get close and inhale the fumes and play 'let's identify the marque'. We studied a map of the route and chose our viewing point beside a traffic-light controlled crossroads that we hoped might afford us the best views of cars both stationary and racing.

That was the theory. In practice, the junction was actually being controlled by a bouncy little chap in a peaked cap and overlong trousers with two deadly weapons, a piercing pea-whistle and a sort of lolly-stick for pointing at vehicles and waving them through.

He practised his technique a few times on the normal local traffic (if there is anything 'normal' about any type of Italian traffic) and there were only a few near misses, no actual crashes, so by the time the race cars started appearing, Carlo the Controller was confidently in command.

Cars, lorries, scooters, motorbikes and pedal cycles bore down on him from all directions but Carlo could halt them in their tracks with one well-aimed flap of his stick.

A few of the local drivers, unaware of what was happening and how huge and significant this day was in their village's history, noticed nothing untoward and drifted over the crossroads in the same heedless manner they had probably done for the past 60 years. Carlo remained calm, shrugged a bit, and turned his concentration to a row of heavy-breathing pantechnicons that he would not allow to pass until he gave the drivers the nod. Oh Carlo, the power vested in you, your hat and your lolly stick!

The simmering chaos on the road was replicated beside us on the pavement, where grown-ups, children and, inexplicably, dogs, threaded around each other as they sought the best vantage points.

At last, everyone settled down and the first cars started to appear. Carlo seemed so vulnerable out there in the middle, alternately flapping, bouncing and whistling like a furious football referee. I worried for him as wave after wave of Ferrari supercars bore down on him, their thunderous roar splitting the air and making the ground shake. These were the glamorous outriders, leading the way like overdressed, noisy, show-offs.

Carlo got them all through unscathed, and then the classic cars began their more sedate but no less thrilling passage past us. After two hours they were still coming, wave after glorious wave of them, their occupants waving to us, their adoring, starstruck admirers.

By the time David and I left we were sated with the thrill and spectacle of it all. And Carlo? I reckon he must have got home that night a dust-encrusted, fume-raddled wreck, his nerves strung to the point of exhaustion, his lips sore from blasting that whistle, his arm aching from flapping the lolly-stick.

What a good job well done, Carlo. I do hope we weren't the only ones to appreciate what a hero you were.

Valiant and vulnerable: Carlo keeps the Mille Miglia moving.

Digestivo

Have we reached the end of the line for Brits buying holiday homes in Italy? As I write this early in 2017, we are reeling from the global financial meltdown, the collapse of the property market in Italy, the continuing Italian political instability, the Brexit vote to leave the European Union, the devastating earthquakes in central Italy . . . so is the British obsession with buying in Italy a thing of the past? Were we among the last to have the full experience of buying a wreck in Le Marche, having it restored and enjoying it? Is it now only for the seriously wealthy or for people prepared to swap the glories of Le Marche and its neighbours for a less beautiful but more seismically stable area?

It would certainly seem as though the days when you could snap up a run-down house and an acre or two of land for a pittance have passed but, like everywhere, market forces call the tune. If foreign buyers are no longer prepared to risk big money, property values in Italy may carry on sinking until they become tempting again - and the whole adventure could begin anew. Time will tell.

22539307R00112

Printed in Great Britain
by Amazon